Graham Cooke

Qualities of a
Spiritual Warrior

Victory is staying fresher longer.

Graham

An Interactive Journal

WAY OF THE WARRIOR Series ... 1

Brilliant Book House LLC
6391 Leisure Town Road
Vacaville, California 95687
U.S.A.
www.brilliantbookhouse.com

Requests for information should be addressed to:

Graham Cooke
office@grahamcooke.com

ISBN 978-1-934771-02-0

Endorsements

Any sustained move of God calls forth a three fold cord that cannot quickly be torn apart. These cords woven together include the Power of God, the Character of God and the Wisdom Ways of God. Graham Cooke draws on his years of ministry experience to bring us needed insight in his series *The Way of the Warrior*. The spirit of wisdom rests upon this man and will come upon you as you partake. Read and heed the lessons!

James W. Goll
Encounters Network
Author of The Lost Art of Intercession, The Seer,
The Coming Prophetic Revolution and many more

Life on planet earth offers the most wonderful challenges, inviting us to taste glorious victory as we overcome with faith and love. The nature of a true warrior in the Kingdom is both created and seasoned through the responses of such virtues in the midst of resistance, offense, and persecution. *The Way of the Warrior* will not only impart encouragement to those of you who are in the midst of trials and testings but it will also actually cause you to hunger for the very things that will establish you in the highly honored position of a true warrior of God. Warriors of God, know the ways of God. Graham Cooke pens this work with mastery and restful authority... because he truly lives *the way of the warrior.*

Patricia King
xpmedia.com

"Qualities of a Spiritual Warrior" is the most inviting book on the subject I've ever seen. It is refreshing to read a book on warfare where the author is not impressed with the devil. Graham instead restores us to our rightful place of being captivated with Jesus. His wonderful understanding of the ways of the Kingdom does more than just bring clarity, it empowers the believer to live with victory as the normal expression of following Christ.

Bill Johnson
Bethel Church, Redding, CA
Author - When Heaven Invades Earth

Spiritual warriors who forcefully advance the kingdom by intentionally invading enemy territory attract the heat of principalities and powers and soon find themselves in hand to hand combat with these dark spirit beings. But the 'wisdom of the battlefield' belongs to these warriors and even the principalities and powers stand in awe at the unveiling of the manifold wisdom of God. (Ephesians 3:10) Like Caleb, Graham's appetite for battle continues to grow and these pages reveal the wisdom that only comes through seasoned frontline spiritual warfare. As Solomon once said; "By wise counsel wage war." (Proverbs 20:18)

Phil Mason
Spiritual Director, New Earth Tribe
Byron Bay, Australia

Dedication

The first time I really noticed Theresa was in Sacred Space, an evening at The Mission, solely dedicated to worship and intimacy. She danced with complete abandonment, like nobody else existed except Jesus. In the ensuing months I heard her pray like a warrior. She went after the enemy with a passion. I was struck by her sparkle, though she carried the marks of suffering.

She intrigued me. I made it my business to get to know her. When the time was right for both of us, I carefully pursued her. There is a longer version to this tale. Suffice it to say that I married her and could not be happier.

I dedicate this book to my wife and her passion for all things Jesus. She is a blonde, petite, beautiful tornado; and I love her.

Acknowledgements

Brilliant Book House may be my brainchild, but it is the story of several people in particular. There is Scott Cave of Rook Technologies who designed the website and makes us tick like a 21st century timepiece. Then there is Jordan Bateman: a good friend, genius, all around good guy, and a brilliant journalist. Jordan is my pre-editorial magician who takes a CD and knocks it into a working manuscript — amazing.

Jeanne Thompson, my personal assistant, who types the completed works, looks after the office, runs my schedule and makes me laugh. She is a New Yorker from Queens ... enough said.

Thank you to Sophie Patten for her hard work on researching and compiling materials and for her proofing and editing skills. She does it with such obvious dedication, great kindness and some humor!

The BBH staff, consisting of Kellie, Matt and Lisa are great to have around, they are funny, committed, hard working and a great team.

What can I say. I'm blessed to have these people on the team. We may be small in number but not in stature. Together, we punch above our weight. Move over Goliath, or lose some teeth.

Invocation

Father, thank you that this is our time and season to fight back — to war against a religious spirit that has bound up your people in legalism, judgment, and an earthly logic that prevents discovery of the realm of Your Spirit.

Thank you that we can war against a religious system that teaches rules, performance and duty but does not allow us to have ongoing encounters with the Living God.

Thank you that we have a joyful, legal right, because of Christ's sacrifice, to wage war on the enemy wherever we may find him. Thank you for favor and vengeance combined. That, in our freedom in Christ, you not only deliver us from being victims but you give us a ministry in the very areas where we have been robbed and ashamed.

Everyone that we in turn set free is a sign of our payback on the enemy. To destroy the works of the devil is the evidence of Your power at work.

I pray that You would give us a spirit of wisdom and revelation in the knowledge of Jesus. That you would cause our eyes to be opened into enlightenment of the glory of Heaven here on earth. On earth as it is in Heaven — no more, no less.

Be our tutor, lead us into a revelatory experience of the power of the Christ-life within. In His Name and for His glory. Amen.

Contents
Qualities of the Spiritual Warrior

The World is Crying Out for Heroes

Every culture has its icons—legends who become larger than life as their story is told and retold. In days past, these heroes have often been war and political figures whose images are burned in our mind's eye. In western nations like Great Britain, the United States, and Canada, we can picture them clearly: Winston Churchill — under fire from every side, chomping on his cigar, face resolute, certain his nation would not fall. (Who can forget his "We will fight them on the beaches," speech which so wonderfully armed a people with resolve and determination to both endure and overcome?); George Washington — standing in his boat as he crossed the Delaware River, tunic flapping in the breeze; American soldiers, raising the flag at Iwo Jima; William Wallace, running through the Scottish highlands; General Douglas MacArthur — smoking his corn cob pipe, defiantly promising, "I shall return."; Admiral Nelson at Trafalgar; Wellington, defeating Napoleon at Waterloo; the ragtag band of Canadians, overcoming all odds to take Vimy Ridge.

As the western world has evolved, we have seen our cultural heroes shift from revolutionary warriors to sports figures and entertainers. Their images resonate with us as well. Michael Jordan, flying through the air, tongue hanging out, ready to tomahawk the ball through the hoop. John Elway, juking and jiving and plunging head first into the end zone. Wayne Gretzky ducking out from behind the net and lifting a backhanded shot past a hapless goaltender. Roger Clemens striking out batter after batter after batter. Muhammad Ali flexing his muscles over a splayed-out Sonny Liston. Entertainment has provided similar icons: Bono, arms spread open, singing with all his might; Marlon Brando as *Godfather* Vito Corleone; Russell Crowe, the *Gladiator* himself, shouting to the crowd "Are you not entertained?"; Jerry, George, Elaine, and Kramer chatting away at the coffee shop on *Seinfeld;* Batman standing alone atop a building.

But these icons pale in comparison to the influence of spiritual heroes. The lives of these war heroes and entertainment superstars have been examined and chronicled, but never to the degree of the heroes of the Bible. An entertainer's life is like dust compared to the influence of those who accomplished great things for the Kingdom of God. For centuries, people have looked to the lives of these spiritual heroes for guidance and inspiration. How did they do it? How did someone like that change the world?

Hebrews 11, one of my favorite passages of Scripture, lists some of these spiritual heroes. It leaves us a defining image of their greatness. Abel, who offered *"a more excellent sacrifice"* than his brother Cain, and who had *"God testifying of his gifts"* (verse 4). Enoch, who *"pleased God"* to the point that he did not die, but *"was taken away"* by Him (verse 5). Noah, who *"moved with godly fear"* and became *"heir of the righteousness which is according to faith"* (verse 7). Abraham, who *"went out, not knowing where he was going,"* because he had a promise from God (verse 8). Sarah, his wife, who *"bore a child when she was past the age, because she judged Him faithful who had promised"* (verse 11).

Isaac, Jacob, Joseph, Moses, Rahab, Gideon, Barak, Samson, Jephthah, David, Samuel, and the prophets: heroes all of them. *"Through faith, [they] subdued kingdoms, worked righteousness, obtained promises, stopped the mouths of lions, quenched the violence of fire, escaped the edge of the sword, out of weakness were made strong, became valiant in battle, turned to flight the armies of the aliens,"* as Hebrews 11:33-34 says. And for every one mentioned in this passage, there are five more left off the list. A new generation of spiritual heroes fills the pages of the New Testament: Peter, the rock on which Christ built His church; John, the Beloved, resting his head on Jesus' shoulder; the Apostle Paul, preaching the Gospel fearlessly—even while in chains; John the Baptist, foretelling the arrival of the Messiah; Mary, the gentle and devoted mother of a Child that changed everything; Barnabas, the encourager; Timothy, the young pastor; Luke, the faithful scribe and doctor.

Who can ever forget at a critical time in the life of black Americans, Martin Luther King standing resolutely against separatism and declaring, "I have a dream".

11

Think of the enormous respect from all people and creeds for the purity and passion of Billy Graham, a man after God's heart. My own heroes are: Graham Perrins, who taught me prophetics and gave me a profound love of scripture; Arthur Burt, Harry Greenwood, and Ian Andrews who modeled a life of faith and a passion for the Spirit; Gerald Coates, for his courage in standing up for non-religious Christianity; Paul Pillai, an unsung apostolic, church planting hero in India; Mike Bickle and his passion for intimacy with God.

For all the people in prophetic ministry who have stood the test of time and the warfare that surrounds their life and have prevailed over the enemy and especially organized religion —John Paul Jackson, Rick Joyner, Jim Goll, Larry Randolph, Bob Jones, Patricia King, Stacey Campbell.

All of them, all of them, icons and legends in their own fields. The list of Hebrews 11 is ongoing in the Father's heart.

This is the legacy that we as Christians walk in. As the poet John McCrae said in his work, *In Flanders' Fields*, "Take up our quarrel with the foe: To you from failing hands we throw the torch; be yours to hold it high." The heroes of the faith have passed this torch from generation to generation, and now it is time for our present-day spiritual warriors to carry it forward. We are heirs of the same Christ that these heroes prophesied would come and redeem the world.

Assignment

- ❊ Who are your heroes and why? Identify them by name and consider what they have been to you.
- ❊ How has their life touched yours?
- ❊ What difference have they meant to:
    - ❊ Your walk with God
    - ❊ Your ministry and place in the Kingdom
    - ❊ The relationships around your life

Commission

- ❊ Write to these people to bless, encourage and affirm them in their calling and destiny.
- ❊ If your hero is deceased, write a letter to the Father asking for similar qualities to be in you.

Personal Notes

Spiritual Warriors Change Atmospheres

Every Christian is called at the very least to be a soldier in the army of God. Soldiers are called to counter evil with the overwhelming, overcoming good that flows from a heart in love with God. No matter what situation a Christian soldier is in, they must live from their spirit. Soldiers bless everyone around them and contribute to a positive spiritual atmosphere.

The devil is the "prince of the power of the air" [Ephesians 2:2]. He lives in the atmosphere! He operates to change the climate of faith into unbelief. He seeks to alter the mood of people away from the fruit of the Spirit to something more negative and sinister. He desires to be our substitute for God; therefore to make us like him. Anytime he can release our flesh instead of our true spirit, he has achieved a purpose, however temporary.

The enemy knows that he doesn't have to beat the church, just deflect her from her own God-given destiny. A people without inheritance have no substance. For people to grow properly we must first change the atmosphere and then create a new environment that produces people of quality, not just quantity.

"It is for freedom that Christ has set us free" [Galatians 5:1]. Any church, ministry, or leadership that is not releasing people into their own destiny, identity, and inheritance cannot produce a warrior; and possibly, not even a soldier.

Warriors stoke the atmosphere. They inflame passion by the way they live their own lives. What you are in your own destiny you exhibit quite naturally. Warriors are unconscious models of a kingdom that is far above all principalities and powers.

The first stage of warfare is to change the atmosphere around us where we live, work, and worship. We do that by releasing as much of the blessing of God as possible, each day. We are ambassadors of reconciliation representing a joyful, gracious, merciful King who has paid the price for freedom and blessing to be bestowed on all people at all times.

This is the Good News. The righteous anger of God against sin has been satisfied by the death of Jesus. Mercy and Truth have kissed each other, and judgment is suspended on earth until the Day of Judgment occurs in the heavens.

Spiritual warriors fight so that all people may receive the blessing of the Good News. We seek to change the atmosphere over people's lives so that they may experience the glorious benevolence of the rule of God. Through our love, joy, and peace, we push aside negativity, unbelief, and selfishness; so that we can pray, prophesy, and spiritually bless everyone with whom we come into contact.

The plan of the enemy is to create misery, take away hope, and develop a climate of despair and helplessness. We overcome evil with good. We must of necessity position ourselves daily in Christ in order to reveal the nature of the Kingdom. Good soldiers fight the space around them to create a clearing where Christ can be seen.

No Christian has an excuse to moan about the enemy. After all, as 1 John 4:4 says, "You are of God, little children, and have overcome them, because He who is in you is greater than he who is in the world". Every soldier should want to be a thorn in the side of the enemy. We can make a difference.

Assignment

- ❈ What is the prevailing atmosphere in your own heart?
- ❈ Identify positive and negative aspects that are currently influencing your view of God, self, others.
- ❈ How will you reinforce your positive mental, emotional, and spiritual internal atmosphere with God?
- ❈ What is the opposite of your current negativity, and how will you allow the Holy Spirit to transform you in these areas?

* In your home church or current spiritual environment, what is the present ruling atmosphere?

Commission

* Working with the Holy Spirit and personal friends, develop an action plan and a strategy to transform your personal and corporate atmospheres.

Personal Notes

Standing in the Forefront of the Battle

Spiritual warriors, however, play a different role than Christian soldiers; they are a completely different breed. They are on special assignment, charged with specific God-led initiatives against the enemy. Spiritual warriors are the special forces of the Kingdom, going out against the enemy in advance of the Church. Out there, they battle and hold ground until Christian soldiers — reinforcements — arrive to help them. They are out in front of that broader force.

Like David's mighty men they are raised up to restore a nation. They fight for higher stakes than the local community. They have a zeal to take a city, a state, a region, a nation. They fight within the political sphere, the judicial system, the world of commerce and social justice to change laws, create legislation that is fair and equal to all.

David's men were identified by their strengths as much as their name: the incredible swordplay of Josheb-basshebeth who killed 800 men at one time; the indomitable courage of Eleazar who, after everyone had retreated, stayed and fought the enemy alone and won against the odds — a great victory; Shammah who defended a piece of ground alone and unaided against a whole troop of Philistines (What a stand!); Abishai could not be overcome by 300 men and won an amazing battle with just a spear; Benaiah killed two lion-like [e.g., ferocious] heroes of Kabzeel — then for fun dropped into a pit on a snowy day to kill a lion! Another time he killed a giant from Egypt using just a club against his spear [2 Samuel 23].

Great leaders produce mighty warriors. These men were not around in the time of Saul, but appeared during the rise and rule of David — a man after God's own heart.

The apostles and Hebrews 11 heroes were the foremost spiritual warriors of their time. They have given us a template for the greatness to which we are called. They took and held ground until God's soldiers of their day could reinforce them. When the teenaged David stepped forward and killed Goliath, his victory inspired the previously paralyzed Israelite soldiers to charge into the fight. When Gideon accepted God's call to lead the fight against the Midianites, others fell in behind—so many, in fact, that God had to whittle down the number. Noah was obedient to God in the days before the flood and saved humanity from extinction, but it was his children that fell in behind and repopulated the earth. Moses and Aaron faced Pharaoh alone, but all of Israel walked across the Red Sea to freedom. Joshua and Caleb spied out the Promised Land, but the entire nation had to take it. Joseph went alone into Egypt, but forged a place for his entire family. Spiritual warriors take the first and most courageous step—but soldiers are needed to come behind them and back them up.

Assignment

❃ What is the current battle in your church?

❃ What is the next step your spiritual community needs to take in alignment with the Holy Spirit?

❃ What, by your attitude, faith and vision, can you do to enable that step to be taken?

Commission

❃ Align yourself with the Holy Spirit. Listen to His heart and affection for the local company of God's people.

❃ Step into the breach and become His hands and voice to effect true transformation.

Personal Notes

Great Leaders Produce Kingdom People

A church that is top-down led — that is not permission giving, — that does not allow the people to dream or encounter God fully for themselves — can never produce a warrior. In truth, people who want more of God are going to leave these inferior houses to seek the Lord and His greatness.

A church that has no concept of or experience in the Kingdom is not fighting on the right battlefield. The church is the place of intimate devotion to the King. A place of fellowship, encouragement, dreaming and development. People are equipped and prepared for a life of destiny. They are released to discover their inheritance, to live in favor, and to move out of abundance — not poverty.

People who are developed specifically to serve another man's ministry can never rise to a place of sonship within that organization. They will only ever be servants to someone's anointing. This type of discipleship arises out of a task oriented, functional paradigm of Christianity that actually can disengage people from their own dreams and disinherit them from God's desire for their life. I have lost count of the times when prophecy has been spoken to an individual in this type of environment, and it has resulted in them being fired from their position because apparently they now no longer "fit" the requirements of the leadership.

In a relational paradigm like the Kingdom, our challenge is to produce sons and fathers who are like the Godhead in personality, character, and anointing. God gives dreams and sends prophets to confirm His desires. Leaders, who are also fathers, are intensely interested and involved in the identity, inheritance, and destiny of the people that the Lord has committed to their charge. Otherwise, we are merely using people.

This is fertile soil that produces warriors and champions for the whole of society not just the world of the church.

One of the most powerful corporate transformations I have ever seen occurred at my own church, The Mission, several years ago. Our senior team leader, David Crone, stood before the congregation and gave them permission to dream. I felt the roof lift off the church and an anointing came down that day that began to transform peoples lives.

Our journey as a congregation had been to rediscover and come under a relational paradigm of friendship, love, and meaningful relationship in line with the Father, Son, and Holy Spirit. We wanted their level of loving interaction, involvement, culture of honor, and teamwork!

Out of that desire we began the process of reshaping the church, and our journey began to change to reflect the growing passion for intimate friendships with God and one another. Our mindsets, culture, and ways of operating began to adjust accordingly. We began to make decisions that defined our identity as we saw it being adjusted by the Spirit. We saw beyond the world of the church and its ministry and discovered the wider anointing and deeper power of the Kingdom.

David's permission released people to dream. As a leadership we are becoming better facilitators, enabling destiny and inheritance to shape people's identity. The prophetic began to grow and become a normal part of our life. We are no longer a church that loves prophecy; we are a prophetic community with a present/future dimension to all that we are and do.

The result of these decisions and that specific permission has been the release of a kingdom presence that has pushed us more into the supernatural realm. Healings, miracles, supernatural gifts, and personal encounters with God are increasing.

David wrote a book, a journal of the events and the road we traveled towards permission. It's a must read for everyone but especially leaders. It is entitled *Decisions That Define Us* and can be purchased on our website www.brilliantbookhouse.com.

Assignment

- Look at the Godhead. What type of relationship exists between the Father, Son and Holy Spirit?
- How can you duplicate that in the relationships around you?

❉ What conversations can begin; what decisions can be made that enable us to shift from a functional paradigm to a relational one?

Commission

❉ Looking at your current leaders and other key people in the church, develop an action plan for the present/future that includes:
  ❉ Kingdom conversations
  ❉ A paradigm shift towards relational Christianity
  ❉ The importance of training, equipping, empowering, and releasing people to fulfill their God-given identity.

Personal Notes

Seeing Beyond the Natural Realm

Elisha was a powerful spiritual warrior in his time, leading the charge against God's enemies. In 2 Kings 6, he single-handedly stopped the king of Syria from defeating Israel. The prophet kept receiving words of knowledge about the Syrians' plan. He even knew what was being said in secret meetings in the king's palace bedroom, as we read in 2 Kings 6:8-9, 11-12—

> *Now the king of Syria was making war against Israel; and he consulted with his servants, saying, "My camp will be in such and such a place." And the man of God sent to the king of Israel, saying, "Beware that you do not pass this place, for the Syrians are coming down there." Therefore the heart of the king of Syria was greatly troubled by this thing; and he called his servants and said to them, "Will you not show me which of us is for the king of Israel?"*
> *And one of his servants said, "None, my lord, O king; but Elisha, the prophet who is in Israel, tells the king of Israel the words that you speak in your bedroom."*

Elisha's close relationship with God made him privy to the plans of the enemy. He heard the most private words of the king in his spirit. The Syrians were incensed—they tried to attack Elisha, but the prophet simply led that army into Israelite territory and turned them over to his own king. Imagine fighting someone like Elisha—you can't kill him, you can't legislate against him, you can't even capture him. He was a thorn in evil's side, just as a spiritual warrior should be.

Spiritual warriors see beyond the natural into a realm of the Spirit where God lives. Elisha saw horses and chariots of fire all around the enemy. He had a level of perception not earthed in natural thinking or logic. "There are more with us, than there are with them," he grinned, as he walked out to meet them — seemingly alone, yet powerfully backed up by Heaven.

Spiritual warriors have access to a different reality than the natural facts. This is what makes them irresistible and irrepressible in the fight. To see from heaven's perspective opens you up to all the claims and desires of heaven in the circumstances of life.

Perceptions are powerful. Perceptions relieve oppression. They release provision. Prophecy arises out of perception. Promises are realized by a people whose awareness of God is greater than their natural vision.

Spiritual warriors stand out in a crisis because they have insight into God's Name and Nature. Intimacy enables us to become preoccupied within our affections.

When we set our heart on someone, our intimacy must go to a deeper level of love and trust. This is as true of human relationships as it is of God.

Insight releases discernment. When we are focused on the real, the false is always exposed. Intimacy cannot be faked. Intimacy intimidates the enemy. There is always intimidation in warfare. Goliath tried it on David:

> *When the Philistine looked and saw David, he disdained him; for he was but a youth, and ruddy, with a handsome appearance.*
>
> *The Philistine said to David, "Am I a dog, that you come to me with sticks?" And the Philistine cursed David by his gods.*
>
> *The Philistine also said to David, "Come to me, and I will give your flesh to the birds of the sky and the beasts of the field."*
>
> *Then David said to the Philistine, "You come to me with a sword, a spear, and a javelin, but I come to you in the name of the LORD of hosts, the God of the armies of Israel, whom you have taunted.*
>
> *"This day the LORD will deliver you up into my hands, and I will strike you down and remove your head from you. And I will give the dead bodies of the army of the Philistines this day to the birds of the sky and the wild beasts of the earth, that all the earth may know that there is a God in Israel,*
>
> *and that all this assembly may know that the LORD does not deliver by sword or by spear; for*

the battle is the LORD'S and He will give you
into our hands."
[1 Samuel 17:42-47]

Out of his own intimacy as a man after God's own heart, David intimidated the giant before him and won an incredible victory that delivered a nation. Saul and his compatriots listened to Goliath and were rendered unequal to the challenge. David knew only one voice. His identity as a warrior was rooted in his intimacy.

Praise is not an option. It is an absolute necessity, like air and water. Your revelation of God must result in a praise proclamation against the enemy. In worship we declare to God. In warfare we proclaim to the enemy. If we have no personal internal declaration of who God is for us, then we have no external proclamation to fight behind. Spiritual warriors are men and women of passionate intimacy and forceful thanksgiving. They lead with their rejoicing. They inspire the assembly to see God's majesty and to line up for battle knowing the fight belongs to God — victory belongs to us. We fight from victory, not towards it!

Soldiers need to line up behind spiritual warriors in times of crisis. It is in those crises that the purposes of God are most forcefully advanced. If we had just a few spiritual warriors stand up in every church in the land, nothing would stop the Kingdom. Only a very small number of spiritual warriors are needed to break through in a region.

A spiritual warrior is someone who can kill a thousand of the enemy without blinking an eye. Unfortunately, our churches are full of people too anemic to kill anything! But one or two warriors can change all that. The men and women listed in Hebrews 11 and other passages of Scripture first broke through for themselves and then led everyone else into that same dynamic place in the spirit.

What remarkable people those warriors were; Scripture records that *"the world was not worthy"* of them (Hebrews 11:38). Spiritual warriors make tough choices, confidently, about who, how, and where they will focus their internal attention. They live from the inside—funneling the energy and revelation they receive from the Holy Spirit out into the world. They punch through spiritual opposition, allowing soldiers to pour in and occupy new territory.

Assignment

* Think about your current level of intimacy with the Lord.
* What needs to improve and increase in your praise, rejoicing and giving thanks?
* What does living from the inside out mean to you?
* What particular insight of God do you need in order to combat your present circumstances?

Commission

❋ Cultivate that insight into a place of forceful rejoicing and thanksgiving.

❋ Produce a declaration of Who God is for you now!

❋ develop a proclamation that you can use on the enemy.

Personal Notes

Difference Between Anger and Assertiveness

Spiritual warriors are not aggressive; they are assertive in a powerful way. When you partake of the nature of God you cannot be angry in the way you once were. It takes a lot for God to get angry, he is very slow in this regard. If He does get angry, it's momentary and always for a specific purpose that produces good eventually.

When most people get angry they mostly assert the unredeemed side of their personality, what we term as our flesh or the old nature. That is because we have one nature learning how to submit to another. On days our heart can be divided. Our anger can be unreasoning and spiteful.

God has no such problem in His personality. He is infinite, eternal, and unchangeable. In our experience, anger is an emotion representing a change in one's reaction. In that particular sense, God does not become angry. He only appears to do so in the eyes of men.

"Be angry and sin not" [Ephesians 4:26] is how the Father works. It takes an incredible amount to make Him angry because His patience is overwhelmingly brilliant. His goodness, kindness, gentleness, love, peace, and joy are all so huge that any anger can only ever be momentary; and then the beauty of His nature floods back into our relationship with Him.

In the new covenant of Christ within, and us living in Christ, God's anger is assuaged by sacrifice. He poured out all of His anger on Jesus and now has none left. God's anger has always been developmental — necessary chastisement to enable His people to learn more effectively. A step on the way to full maturity. A short, sharp shock that brings us up short and makes us think about things a little harder.

Of course there have been occurrences when the anger of God has been combined with His people fully reaping what they sow. In those instances, anger can look like punishment, but it isn't. Discipline without development is punishment.

In the case of Israel not being permitted to enter Canaan the first time, we see that Israel had learned nothing from four hundred years of slavery. Her rebellion and disobedience had resulted in being overcome by the enemy and taken captive.

The same obstinate characteristics prevented her from being free and inheriting the promise. The options available were:

     a)   allow them to enter Canaan where they would be killed because their rebellion makes them vulnerable in warfare …

     b)   allow them to return to Egypt and an oppressor who will slaughter them because of the plagues and to teach other nations a lesson about usurping Egyptian authority…

c) stay in the wilderness with God who will feed and clothe you, while a younger generation is learning how to walk with God properly.

In discipline, God stays present. He committed Himself to forty years of Presence in the wilderness with the whole of Israel, in order to teach a younger Israel how to be with Him. God's chosen anger is developmental and only occurs when we have repeatedly not given ourselves to learning about fellowship. His anger is always a last resort. He will not always strive with the heart of man [Genesis 6:3]. The Father has this incredible, astonishing ability to be longsuffering towards humanity. That doesn't mean He is permanently sad. There are no tears in heaven. The Father's personal joy is so all embracing it covers everything, just as His love covers a multitude of sins. His longsuffering is immersed in His joy (Colossians 1:11] and we can be the same. The Father's ability to love combined with His joy in Himself is the cornerstone of our relationship with Him. His goodness, kindness, gentleness, mercy, patience, faithfulness, grace, and self-control all combine to become longsuffering with joy. Paul's words in 1 Corinthians 13:4-8a is descriptive of God's nature.

> *Love is patient, love is kind and is not jealous;*
> *love does not brag and is not arrogant, does not*
> *act unbecomingly; it does not seek its own, is*
> *not provoked, does not take into account a*

> *wrong suffered, does not rejoice in*
> *unrighteousness, but rejoices with the truth;*
> *bears all things, believes all things, hopes all*
> *things, endures all things. Love never fails.*

His anger is not a reaction to our sin, it's a response that aids our development. He has this intense desire that we should share in His holiness. Righteousness, the lifestyle of thinking, speaking, doing, and living in a holy manner, is a key part of our walk with God. We need training in holiness. Discipline and chastisement are two necessary tools that He uses so that we may learn the peaceful fruit of righteousness.

> *and you have forgotten the exhortation which is*
> *addressed to you as sons,*
> *"MY SON, DO NOT REGARD LIGHTLY THE*
> *DISCIPLINE OF THE LORD, NOR FAINT WHEN YOU*
> *ARE REPROVED BY HIM;*
> *FOR THOSE WHOM THE LORD LOVES HE*
> *DISCIPLINES, AND HE SCOURGES EVERY SON*
> *WHOM HE RECEIVES."*
> *It is for discipline that you endure; God deals*
> *with you as with sons; for what son is there*
> *whom his father does not discipline?*
> *But if you are without discipline, of which all*
> *have become partakers, then you are*
> *illegitimate children and not sons.*
> *Furthermore, we had earthly fathers to*
> *discipline us, and we respected them; shall we*

*not much rather be subject to the Father of
spirits, and live?*
*For they disciplined us for a short time as
seemed best to them, but He disciplines us for
our good, so that we may share His holiness.
All discipline for the moment seems not to be
joyful, but sorrowful; yet to those who have
been trained by it, afterwards it yields the
peaceful fruit of righteousness.*
[Hebrews 12:5-11]

Everyone one of us needs discipline in our lives.
Self-control is an admirable part of our development
process: living in a vulnerable way before the Holy
Spirit; being God-conscious before the Father as Jesus
lived - "I only say what the Father is saying; I only do
what the Father is doing."; having our hearts fixed on
Jesus [Hebrews 12:1-2] is the only way to live.

The worst thing we can do to our children —
apart from not loving and believing in them — is not to
shape their lives in a disciplined manner. There is no
greatness apart from self-control. Development that
does not include personal government will only
guarantee our mediocrity.

God's chastisement is not anger-based, but
motivated by His passion for our greatness. Similarly,
spiritual warriors save all their anger for the enemy.
They live to destroy the works of the devil. When they
see God's people trapped in sin, religious practices, and
unbelief, they do not rage against the people. Like Jesus

they have a compassion that asserts itself but also a directness of speech and action that engages people with God. We come to set prisoners free — not sentence the warden and the prison guards.

It is vital that spiritual warriors understand the difference between anger and assertiveness. In discipline, God is asserting His holiness so that we might share in it with Him [Hebrews 12:10]. In warfare, we are hugely assertive against the enemy. If we have too much aggression from here, it may be turned against us. Our authority must stem from our submission to God, not from our internal anger. Anger that comes from the soul can be tracked back to it, making us vulnerable to a counter attack.

"Submit therefore to God. Resist the devil and he will flee from you" [James 4:7].

We cannot use our own soul against the enemy. Our soul must be submitted to our own spirit that is mingling with the Holy Spirit in our inner man. Being led by the Spirit means we only do things the way God wants them done. Submission is where we make ourselves vulnerable to the goodness of God. Submission is a joyful act of surrender to a beloved Sovereign for His own purposes. The enemy cannot stand against that act of loving abandonment.

The first rule of warfare is that we cannot take ground from the enemy if he has ground in us. Cleaning and clearing our own house is a vital part of our own self-control and personal discipline. God works in us and through us, and it is important that we know the difference. Otherwise we will project our own development needs onto others. "In me first", was the Apostle Paul's principle for development [1 Timothy 1:16].

Assignment

* What is the Lord currently talking to you about in your personal life?
* What area of self-control do you need to exhibit next?
* What is the difference between aggression and assertiveness?

Commission

* What are you learning about the anger of the Lord and His unchanging nature?
* Write down some key thoughts on that subject and share them with a friend!

Personal Notes

Rest: The Warrior's Greatest Weapon

It is not violence that propels these spiritual warriors forward. Ironically, they break through enemy lines through their own ability to rest in the Lord. These mighty men and women live in a state of untroubled calm and rest despite every annoyance thrown their way. While the enemy dishes out chaos and accusation, spiritual warriors are anchored by the inner life of the spirit.

Rest is a weapon. As Christians, we should be incredibly peaceful, tranquil, and calm. The enemy cannot penetrate the armor of a person at rest in God. Spiritual warriors know that part of their inheritance is complete confidence in Him. This confidence in His nature puts their spirit at rest. All of God's promises are designed to inspire us in our dependence on Him. We are completely reliant on His grace and mercy. All we can do is joyfully and humbly live in that revelation no matter what comes against us.

As we see in Hebrews 11, Scripture is full of examples where ordinary people ran while warriors stayed and fought until they broke through. But to stay when everyone around you is running takes supreme confidence in who God wants to be for you. These warriors carry an assurance of God's heart toward them.

It is not about how strong we are, but how powerful the Lord is in our lives! Spiritual warriors know and have learned how to use their own weakness to become vulnerable to the strength and power of God.

To rest in God's power when your own weaknesses seem to be screaming at you … that's grace! To be confident in who God is for you when you feel overwhelmed by odds against you — that's peace! To stand alone against massive intimidation — that's trust!

To know beyond any shadow of a doubt that God is bigger, and therefore you cannot lose — that's the faith that moves mountains! Spiritual warriors know who God is for them, and they are aware of the partnership they have with Him. This partnership in biblical terms is called a yoke. Jesus used this term in His call to people to enter a rest with Him.

> *Come to Me, all who are weary and heavy-laden, and I will give you rest.*
> *"Take My yoke upon you and learn from Me, for I am gentle and humble in heart, and YOU WILL FIND REST FOR YOUR SOULS.*
> *"For My yoke is easy and My burden is light."*
> *[Matthew 11:28-30]*

There is a place set aside for us in the Spirit where we can make the enemy tired. We can make him weary, discouraged, deflated, and intimated by our intimacy and our rest in Jesus. On earth as it is in heaven. Is there any weariness of soul in heaven? Is there any mental tiredness or emotional depression? These things have been bound because joy and rest have been loosed!

The promise of rest instead of weariness is a huge gift from Jesus!

> *"Peace I leave with you; My peace I give to you; not as the world gives do I give to you. Do not let your heart be troubled, nor let it be fearful."*
> *[John 14:27]*

All our overcoming stems from the joy and peace in believing. The Internal Presence of God enables us to overcome the external pressures of life and warfare. Jesus has already overcome these external forces.

> *Who will separate us from the love of Christ? Will tribulation, or distress, or persecution, or famine, or nakedness, or peril, or sword? Just as it is written,*
> *"FOR YOUR SAKE WE ARE BEING PUT TO DEATH ALL DAY LONG;*
> *WE WERE CONSIDERED AS SHEEP TO BE SLAUGHTERED."*
> *But in all these things we overwhelmingly conquer through Him who loved us.*
> *[Romans 8:35-37]*

It is important to note here, that the victory of Jesus does not shield us from the intrusion and impact of adversity and warfare. Nor does it mean that we will not suffer or even lose our life in the service of God.

> *but in everything commending ourselves as servants of God, in much endurance, in afflictions, in hardships, in distresses,*

in beatings, in imprisonments, in tumults, in
labors, in sleeplessness, in hunger,
in purity, in knowledge, in patience, in
kindness, in the Holy Spirit, in genuine love,
in the word of truth, in the power of God; by
the weapons of righteousness for the right hand
and the left,
by glory and dishonor, by evil report and good
report; regarded as deceivers and yet true;
as unknown yet well-known, as dying yet
behold, we live; as punished yet not put to
death,
as sorrowful yet always rejoicing, as poor yet
making many rich, as having nothing yet
possessing all things. [2 Corinthians 6:4-10]

What it means is that despite what happens to us, victory is guaranteed as we remain in the faithfulness of God. There may be a larger objective to achieve than the preservation of our own life. Our personal objective is always the glory of God. To achieve the privilege of presenting glory to God we need three things working together: Firstly, we need to be able to stand joyfully in the blood of Jesus — to know its power for us over the enemy, and to rejoice in it. Secondly, we need to proclaim our own personal testimony regarding the nature of God in the face of all opposition. Thirdly, we need to love the life of Jesus more than our own so that we are never preoccupied with self preservation. [Revelation 12:11]

The one who overcomes in this manner, receives blessings in heaven that are astronomical privileges for eternity. [Revelation 3:21]

Victory — the purpose of God being achieved **through** our circumstances — is always present in Christ [2 Corinthians 2:14; 1 Corinthians 15:17]. He has overcome the world and all of its pressures, oppositions and warfare. He has disarmed the ruling powers; thoroughly humiliating them in the process and displaying His power over them for all to see [Colossians 2:15]. Jesus now sits in the place of supreme authority with everything being subject to Him, and His Lordship being evident in and through His body on earth. [Ephesians 1:21-23]

Peace comes in the context of God's overcoming nature displayed to us in Christ. Jesus is supremely unworried. Peace enables us to lead an untroubled life. That is, when trouble comes we are not fazed by it. We know how to live above it in our spirit. We know how to calmly see through it to determine the purpose of God. We are not subject to the pressure of events because we allow His peace to encourage us.

Spiritual warriors have courage because they have peace. We do not let our hearts be troubled, nor are we subject to fear. We believe in God, we know Who Jesus is for us [John 14 1:27]. We rest in the overcoming nature of Jesus.

We don't have to understand everything in detail so that we are at peace. We are governed by peace to such an extent that it rules in our hearts, not our minds [Colossians 3:15]. Peace does not come through settled thinking, but it can be displaced by an anxious, fearful mindset.

Peace comes from our heart — the inner man of the Spirit, our secret place where God lives within. Then it moves out of our heart to guard our mind. Peace dominates our heart and governs our thinking [Philippians 4:7], enabling us to take any negative thoughts captive and destroy unhelpful speculations [2 Corinthians 10:5] that make us prone to weariness and dejection.

The heart of the invitation of Jesus in [Matthew 11:28-30] is for us to take His yoke upon ourselves. A yoke is a partnership relationship that enables us to fully cooperate with Christ in the matter of rest. A young ox is yoked with a more mature ox so that it can be discipled in the role that it will occupy. So with us; we take all of our leads from Jesus. His responses now become our responses as we submit to His intention and power.

Being led by the Spirit arises out of our union with Jesus. "As He is, so are we in this world" [1 John 4:17]. He that is in us is too powerful and much greater than anything or anyone we may meet in life [1 John 4:4]. This yoke relationship is of paramount importance to our rest and peace.

Some people are unequally yoked to a negative. Whenever we allow ourselves to become negative we have been shifted from faith and obedience to a contrary place where it is possible for us to deny, oppose, and resist the promises, goodness, and power of God. We become our own worst enemy. If we are not consciously partnering with God, who are we in alliance with? Jesus said, "He who is not with me, is against me" [John 12:30]. Clearly this can occur at many levels. We cannot resist the grace of God without suffering consequences. Negativity neutralizes faith and nullifies our peace and rest, making us vulnerable to fear, anxiety, doubt, and unbelief. If we find it easy to be cynical, we have already traveled a long way down this road of negative thinking.

If we are prone to being pessimistic or gloomy, our thinking and rest have already been compromised. If our sense of humor is rooted in sarcasm that wounds people [rather than the gentle joshing of a loving friendship], then we have lost the heart of God and need to recover ourselves. If we have become unenthusiastic about Jesus or uninterested in spiritual things, we have possibly been taken captive in our heart and mind.

Being unequally yoked to a negative causes a reversal of favor and leads to stress and difficulty. We lose our heaven sent confidence in Jesus and find ourselves out of position in the Spirit.

Spiritual warriors never allow this to happen to them. Indeed they know that rest is a weapon to be used on the evil one. Rest allows us time and space to wait on the Lord even in the most trying of circumstances. The enemy seeks to pull us out of rest by getting us to act too quickly to events. When we allow that, we are reacting to the situation and not responding to the Lord. Resting and waiting on the Lord is not inactivity — it allows confidence to come through positive reinforcement of our identity in Christ and His inheritance in us.

Spiritual warriors wait. They know that confidence comes from the Lord. His joy is a source of strength. "Be of good cheer. I have overcome the world," echoes in their heart and mind. Warriors give assurance to the weak around them because they themselves operate in a dimension where access to God provides a guaranteed outcome of victory. They rest in that assurance because they fight from victory, not towards it.

These warriors are absolutely positive that God will help them. They are convinced that He is incapable of letting them down. Such thoughts never enter their minds—they are completely focused on the fact that God will save them. In times of warfare and adversity, they have the courageous boldness to stand firm in God.

This confidence enables a spiritual warrior to hold their nerve and be fearless in the face of any attack. They live in the growing conviction that the Lord is pouring out His extravagant delight and affection on them. Everything that is in God, is for these people: "Surely I will help you," He says.

These generous promises are the foundation upon which God would have us approach Him. They are a pathway to Him, reminding us of our utter dependence on His nature. This, in turn, provokes the proper attitude and outlook we need in order to access those promises. We are expected by Him—and received by Him.

"For the LORD will be your confidence, and will keep your foot from being caught," says Proverbs 3:26. God is the most powerful ally in the universe, and a spiritual warrior keeps that fact in mind at all times. We stand before God the same way a much-loved son or daughter stands before his or her father. There is no fear or worry, only the love and confidence that comes with being your dad's beloved child. We are totally accepted and have complete access.

God is very confident in Himself; He never doubts anything He is doing. It is this confidence that He seeks to build into the people He touches with His grace.

Assignment

- ❈ Are there negatives in your own life that the Spirit is seeking to change into a more faith-filled perspective?
- ❈ If so, isolate the negatives and examine them. What would be the opposite spirit to them?

* Write that down and practice renewing your insight and thinking until it is adjusted.

Commission

* Think about the areas where by habit you have become prone to negativity.
* What does it mean for you to set peace as a guard in your mind and heart so that negativity is denied entry?
* Practice pushing away a negative, taking poor thoughts captive, renewing your mind with the help of the Holy Spirit.

Personal Notes

Stillness

The ability to still the clamor within our heart and mind is a key part of a spiritual warrior's character. To be quiet in God, even in the face of adversity, is a challenge. But warriors cannot move out of panic; they must operate out of peace and rest.

Demons can roar, people can scream, panic can reign, but peace can live in every one of us and break the power of darkness. When we allow ourselves to relax in that peaceful embrace of God, we learn more about being confident in His great strength.

As we develop this understanding of resting in Him, God will send us into places where only His grace can protect us. This is the astonishing and breathtaking call of a spiritual warrior—to go where others fear to tread, but to take that ground with the confidence of God in us. He calls us to a Luke 10:3-9 existence—

> *Go your way; behold, I send you out as lambs among wolves. Carry neither money bag, knapsack, nor sandals; and greet no one along the road. But whatever house you enter, first say, 'Peace to this house.' And if a son of peace is there, your peace will rest on it; if not, it will return to you. And remain in the same house, eating and drinking such things as they give, for the laborer is worthy of his wages. Do not go from*

*house to house. Whatever city you
enter, and they receive you, eat such
things as are set before you. And heal
the sick there, and say to them, 'The
kingdom of God has come near to you.'*

A spiritual warrior is sent out as a lamb among wolves—but our best friend is a Lion. His all-consuming power turns our puny hearts into a fortress that cannot be taken.

God taught me this principle in an open vision I had many years ago. In the vision, I saw an army of hideous, marauding enemies charging toward me. They were beasts—ugly, twisted, vile beings. Naturally, I began to panic. Suddenly, a curtain came down around me. It surrounded me like a circle; I could only dimly make out the shapes of the enemy on the other side of it.

Inside that small excluded zone, I felt God put His arms around me. From outside the curtain, I could hear the enemy rant and rave, threatening me with every bit of malevolence in his being. The army was violently rampaging, but I had the arms of God around me. In my left ear, I could hear the Lord gently chuckle. "Listen to that," He whispered.

To be embraced by God's kindness in the midst of the fury and crazed curses of the enemy was a profound experience for me. My King was totally unconcerned about what was happening outside that tiny space. "This is our secret place," He whispered to me. "The enemy will never know where it is. All of this is on the inside of you, Graham. You need to know how to step back into your spirit man and live with Me."

God was calm in the face of fury and His confidence rubbed off on me. God's presence in that moment taught me everything I needed to know about standing firm in Him. This quiet confidence gave me the strength and energy to fight on. I could relax in His presence, focusing on Him in quietness. Understanding His statement in Psalm 46:10—"*Be still, and know that I am God,*"–is vital to the development of a spiritual warrior.

God will speak more to a person in silence than He will in conversation; He has a way of inhabiting an environment that speaks volumes.

True stillness involves the destruction of fear because it opens our eyes to the majestic provisions of God on our behalf when everything is against us [Exodus 14 13:14]. In quietness before God we find a confidence, a strength, and a power not available to us outside of stillness [Isaiah 30:15].

Without stillness we cannot see in the Spirit. Experienced fishermen caught in a raging sea were completely undone by the power of the peace of Jesus over the elements. Out of our inner stillness we get to release peace and cause stillness to affect our surroundings [Mark 4:39].

When Elijah was learning stillness, it was for the express purpose that his ability to listen and hear

God's voice could go to a deeper level of perception [1 Kings 19:12-13]. He heard the whisper of God. "A word is brought to us stealthily and our ear receives a whisper of it." [Job 4:12]. The still small voice of God comes to people who learn stillness as a way of life.

The Hebrew word "still" that describes Elijah's experience of God's voice; is the word "dananah", which is itself a derivative of the word "dahan," meaning to be dumbfounded or astonished — literally, to be astonished at the sound.

The power of God in a whisper is overwhelming. Most of the revelation I have received has not come from the study of books, but in a place of meditation — waiting on the Lord. We must practice quietness, because the Lord finds a quiet spirit so irresistible. It gives Him enormous pleasure when we learn stillness and quietness [1 Peter 3:4]. David learned to commune in quietness on his bed [Psalm 4:4].

Spiritual warriors do not react. They revert to their inner place of practical stillness. It is their custom to cultivate rest, peace, and stillness as a way of life before God. Life in the Spirit is one of developing Godly routines that arise out of our spirit when we most need them. We cannot manifest what is not present.

"Be still and know that I am God," [Psalm 46:10] is the best advice you will ever receive on spiritual warfare. Spiritual warriors go into their place of refuge to discover God so that they may exit from the fortress of His presence to combat the enemy.

Assignment

❋ How quiet is your life? How still is your mind? How peaceful are you on difficult days?

❋ What are you hearing and seeing in the Spirit over your own circumstances?

Commission

❋ Write down the above into a simple declaration of peace and stillness and proclaim it to your own heart and mind.

Personal Notes

Boldness and Humility

Scripture and revelation are two key confidence builders in a spiritual warrior's life. God carefully puts His word into our lives to provoke us to look at Him. All too often, we get distracted by His hand, wondering what He is doing. But He wants us to look Him in the eye — to talk with Him, to be with Him. "I want you to see who I am," He says. As Paul wrote in Ephesians 3:12, *"We have boldness and access with confidence through faith in Him."*

Spiritual warriors know how to walk humbly with God, because they understand that they are nothing without His greatness. Humility, however, is not the same as timidity. We do not have to be nervous when we approach God; the sacrifice of Jesus must instead result in a boldness of approach. This confidence in our standing with God should be an unshakable conviction in our hearts. How can we stand outside the throne room when He has swung the door wide open to us? Instead, we must march into His presence. After all, we belong there—because He is there. Jesus has merit, and He has given us His name. We are heirs of God, as explained in Romans 8:12-17—

> *Therefore, brethren, we are debtors— not to the flesh, to live according to the flesh. For if you live according to the flesh you will die; but if by the Spirit you put to death the deeds of the body,*

you will live. For as many as are led by the Spirit of God, these are sons of God. For you did not receive the spirit of bondage again to fear, but you received the Spirit of adoption by whom we cry out, "Abba, Father." The Spirit Himself bears witness with our spirit that we are children of God, and if children, then heirs—heirs of God and joint heirs with Christ, if indeed we suffer with Him, that we may also be glorified together.

Paul continues this thought later in that same chapter (verses 31 through 39)—

What then shall we say to these things? If God is for us, who can be against us? He who did not spare His own Son, but delivered Him up for us all, how shall He not with Him also freely give us all things? Who shall bring a charge against God's elect? It is God who justifies. Who is he who condemns? It is Christ who died, and furthermore is also risen, who is even at the right hand of God, who also makes intercession for us. Who shall separate us from the love of Christ? Shall tribulation, or distress, or persecution, or famine, or nakedness, or peril, or sword? As it is written:

> *"For Your sake we are killed all day*
> *long;*
> *We are accounted as sheep for the*
> *slaughter."*
> *Yet in all these things we are more than*
> *conquerors through Him who loved us.*
> *For I am persuaded that neither death*
> *nor life, nor angels nor principalities nor*
> *powers, nor things present nor things to*
> *come, nor height nor depth, nor any*
> *other created thing, shall be able to*
> *separate us from the love of God which*
> *is in Christ Jesus our Lord.*

Nothing on heaven or earth can separate us from the love of God. Walking humbly in this knowledge means we can come boldly before God. A spiritual warrior doesn't stalk in petulantly or crawl in miserably; he comes with a paradoxical mix of humility in who he is and confidence in who God is.

It is so important to be confident in God — to be unashamed and uncondemned. Grace makes us vulnerable to the majesty of God's lovingkindness toward us. We are a work in progress.

We are learning how to be changed from glory into glory in the likeness of God [2 Corinthians 3:18]. We are moving from that first prime glorious state of salvation to our destiny as manifested sons of the Most High. Each stage we pass through; each season we successfully navigate in the Holy Spirit — more glory is revealed of God's nature that we get to exhibit in Christ. Walking in the Spirit and becoming Christlike are glorious experiences and also experiences of glory.

Confidence is part of the glory of God revealed to us in Christ. As He is, so are we in this world. Boldness and Humility form a beautiful paradox that encapsulates glory. A paradox is two apparently conflicting ideas contained in the same truth. In the matter of our ongoing transformation into becoming Christlike, there are two extremes at work. Firstly, there is how the Father sees us in Christ, as a finished work. Secondly, there is how we see ourselves as we go through the process of change.

God is future/present with us. That is, He deals with us in terms of who we are already in Christ. This is an eternal work and is already completed in Jesus. The Father deals with us through the context of eternity. The Holy Spirit works with us in the context of the here and now. We are present/future with God — in Christ, learning to be Christlike. Jesus stands in the gap between our present and future, interceding for us [Hebrews 7:25].

The Holy Spirit promotes Christ to us and Christ in us as the hope [confident expectation] of glory. In the Father's eyes [seen through the lens of Jesus], we are complete in Christ and welcome in the throne room of His Presence.

"Through Jesus, we have both access in one Spirit to the Father." [Ephesians 2:18] The word "both" means us and Jesus combined, as one! "We can draw near with confidence to the throne of grace, so that we may receive mercy and find grace to help in time of need." [Hebrews 4:16]

We can be bold in our quest for mercy and grace. We can be bold about being in Jesus, and humble about our current place of growth in becoming Christlike. It is a wonderful and unique place of favor in which the Father has placed us before Him. *hona*

He treats us as complete while we are still a work in progress. This means that grace, favor, and inheritance can come to us because of His acceptance of us in the Beloved [Ephesians 1:6], not because of our performance. This alone gives us huge boldness to come before the Father, knowing that He has gifts and favor to bestow upon us as He would bestow them on Jesus.

Humble on earth, confident in heaven. Humble for the present, bold about the future. Bold in the here and now, humbled and awed by who we get to become. We are confident to enter the Holy Place in Christ, and we can do so in full assurance of faith. We are so welcome, accepted, and beloved [Hebrews 10:19-23].

We are learning how to abide in Him so that our confidence is always high, and there is never even a possibility of our being ashamed in His presence. Our hearts can never condemn us because our confidence in the nature of God makes that impossible [1 John 2:28 and 3:21].

Confidence is concerned with certainty! It is about something definite — a firm assurance, a total reliance, an absolute belief, and an unbreakable conviction that provides us with a positive security. There is a yes and amen in God's heart for us!

Assignment

- ❄ In Christ is our starting point. Christ in us is our finishing point. We are a work in progress. What is the Holy Spirit showing you about your own confidence levels in Christ?
- ❄ Explain the difference in your own words between humility and boldness.

Commission

- ❄ Explain what it means to be accepted in the Beloved and complete in Christ; and how the Father loves and provides for you as you become Christlike.
- ❄ Write a short message to a friend about your joy in the Father's love and why you can never be ashamed in His Presence.

Personal Notes

Confidence is the Hallmark

A hallmark is a distinctive feature, signifying excellence. It is the stamp imprinted onto gold and silver that declares its purity, and therefore its value.

Similarly, it is a huge indicator of a spiritual warriors' true worth to the community in which God has placed him. Warriors are people who confidently make choices about where and how to focus from the inner man of the spirit, through the outer man of the soul.

Despite external realities that are adverse and chaotic, spiritual warriors live in a state of untroubled calm and rest by which they are bound to the inner life of the Holy Spirit. They view troublesome, annoying circumstances as opportunities to either defeat the enemy or to practice their own inner spirituality before God. They do not react to events because their focus in training and warfare is to respond to God from their inner man.

They know that part of their inheritance in their walk with God is that they enjoy a complete confidence in Him. They realize that all the promises of God are to enable us to be inspired in our dependence and reliance upon Him. They know that new life events are always followed by an upgrade of God's presence and provision.

Many people get promoted at work or find a new job but never think to upgrade their rest and peace.

A new job or a major change will involve the stress of new people, new learning, larger expectations, and possibly bigger opportunities to fail, as well as succeed. All these can cause pressure not only on us, but also on family. With every new situation there is a fresh provision. The God of peace is with us to bring us into a deeper, broader experience of rest that enables us to overcome [John 14:27; 16:33]. People take on new responsibilities but don't raise their faith to a new level. We battle through circumstances that we feel ill equipped to tackle but do not look for the provision that improves our capacity to receive under pressure.

Many people are unaware that God always uses foresight in His relationship with us. He knows what is coming down the road for us on our journey. He knows where life plots against us. He knows the ambushes of the enemy. He can see the difficult terrain we will have to cross, and He provides for all those eventualities.

People pray as if they are begging God to do them a favor. They forget that He always sees the end from the beginning. He knows all things! The God who knows our journey better than we do has strategically placed a provision next to every problem, obstacle, and opposition — human and demonic. This is called favor.

We rejoice in who God is for us, pray joyfully for the favor that is present, and give thanks for the Father's foresight and intentionality. This is being led by the Spirit.

What you think about God is the most important thought you are ever going to have about anything! How you perceive Him is how you receive Him in your day. We must never have a thought about God that does not magnify His love. He is good; therefore His goodness must be exalted in our thinking. "I would have despaired unless I had believed to see the goodness of the Lord in the land of the living," said David [Psalms 27:13]. This is what it means to be a man after God's own heart, like David. It means that we have a confident expectation of God's nature toward us when circumstances are against us. In difficult situations we seek out God's heart for us now, and we hide in who He is for us. He is our rock, our fortress, and our hiding place.

To step back into His kindness has been my salvation in countless circumstances. That's why God gave me a revelation of His kindness! It is my access point, my doorway into the secret place of His presence. I can escape into His nature for me and live in a higher place than my circumstances. In this way, I get to go through my situations in rest, in faith, and in favor. They become opportunities to overcome something and to declare the nature of God to me personally.

We fight from victory, not towards it. Therefore, we are never staring defeat in the face; the enemy is, when he looks at us. Some obstacles take longer to overcome; in those cases we are also learning about patience and persistence. The point is this —

victory, whether initially or eventually, is never in doubt in our hearts and minds. We focus on God, not the event — the rest is just thinking.

Spiritual warriors joyfully and humbly count on God to come through, no matter what situation they find themselves in. For that to happen, our confidence must first be in God's nature; not just in His power. What is God really, really like? Who is He for you? How do you see His nature, character, and personality?

Every circumstance reveals to you, who God is and what He wants to be for you. This is the first thing that we focus on. In fact, we do not focus on the situation at all, initially; we do that eventually. It's the difference between what is urgent and what is important. Every circumstance has a sound. Difficult situations have a way of clamoring for attention; they have an urgency. However, there is always another sound at work. It's the sound of God speaking in our spirit — the still small voice, the whisper of peace: "I Am is with you;" "I will never leave you nor forsake you;" "Come to Me, I will give you rest."

Why does God whisper in moments like this? It's because He is teaching us to come aside and listen. God is always speaking; warriors are always listening. Never allow the noise of your circumstances to drown out the sound of the Spirit.

Situations are urgent; communion with God is important. The best way to commune is to step out of your circumstances altogether. Step away from them and come to a place of worship, rejoicing, and thanksgiving. If we try to worship in the situation we may not get to a place of breakthrough before God, and the urgency of the event will bring us to prayer too soon. There is a reason why prayer is part of a celebration sandwich.

"Rejoice always; pray without ceasing; in everything give thanks for this is God's will for you in Christ Jesus." [1 Thessalonians 5:16-18]

Real prayer is preceded and followed by a celebration of who God is for us. Majesty is vital when we are in extreme circumstances. We are created to magnify. God put this stamp on all creation: seas roar, trees clap, even the rocks can cry out in exaltation of God. We will magnify; it's in our DNA — even if we magnify the wrong thing.

To magnify means to see something bigger than it actually is in reality. The enemy, through intimidation, always tries to make himself as big as God, to us. He tries to magnify a molehill into a mountain, regarding our circumstances. He wants the problem to become greater than our faith — the pressure, bigger than our peace, the issue to become larger than God's Presence.

To magnify also means to see Someone as big as He really is. To become overwhelmed by God's sovereignty — not in relation to your problem, but in proportion to Who He is in Himself.

The easiest way to separate the problem from the Provider is by putting them in separate places in your heart. I often do this physically, too. I have a room for worship and devotional intimacy and a room for prayer ... in my heart, and in my house. When faced with a problem clamoring for attention — I go into my prayer room (or just another space) and lay the problem down before God. Then I step out of that room, close the door firmly, and go to another room to rejoice and worship.

The act of shutting out a problem in this way enables me to focus my attention fully on the nature of God, and Who He is in Himself — for me. The most important part of every situation is the Presence of God over you and the revelation of God for you in that situation. Whatever you see and hear of God in worship is who you get to become in the situation you find yourself in at that time.

Situations are not just there to resolve. They are allowed, to bring us into a revelation of God and an experience of Him at that point! Our goal is always to become a partaker of Christ.

"We have become partakers of Christ, if we hold fast the beginning of our assurance firm until the end." [Hebrews 3:14]

To be a partaker means we must become engaged and involved in Christ, for Himself. We do not live in our circumstances; we live in Christ. Give Jesus the total pre-eminence of your focus and attention.

Allow the problem to take a lesser place. By shutting it in another room, I am physically free to receive Christ and appropriate Him.

Never focus on the situation. Focus on Jesus. The circumstance is a means to an end. God knows the end that He wants you to receive. There are two of them: firstly, for you to grow into Jesus, using this particular event — for you to become Christlike. And as we partake of Christ, then secondly, we get to partner with the Holy Spirit in the provision of God.

We live in two realms; therefore every situation has two solutions. We live in Heavenly places in Christ; therefore we must put on growth in this dimension. Also, we inhabit the earth; so we must bring from heaven to earth the provision that God has set aside for us. It's called inheritance. On earth, as it is in Heaven.

Spiritual warriors are absolutely convinced that the Lord wants to reveal Himself to them, as well as help them in their circumstances. As I go to another place in my heart (and in my house) I am free to concentrate fully on who God is in Himself. As I rejoice and worship, faith and conviction begin to rise up within me. The Holy Spirit, by His initiative, begins to declare to me the Lord's favor and provision. I can write that down as a crafted prayer[1] or a declaration. Then, when He is ready, I can enter the space where my problem is and begin to pray and declare all that the Father has revealed to me.

Spiritual warriors are totally convinced that the Father is utterly incapable of letting them down. Therefore, in times of warfare and adversity, they draw anointing and power from their own personal crisis and use it to stand with boldness in corporate situations. This enables them to hold their nerve and be fearless in the face of enemy attack. They are partakers of Christ.

What the Father reveals to us in the beginning, will not be the solution to the problem. Firstly, He will show us what we can become in Jesus because we have this situation to empower us [Romans 8:28]. When we see that and receive it, then we get to stand in that as our place before God. We get to put on Christ and hold fast to that revelatory experience all the way through the issue [Hebrews 3:14].

At some point the problem will have to bow to Jesus because of His irrepressible and irresistible nature. This is our contribution to corporate problems and attacks ... warriors supply confidence. We inspire it. We give people a radiant idea of God. Warriors live with a growing conviction that the Lord is delighted to pour out, with extravagant abundance, the certainty of His affection for them. God is disposed to love and care for us.

The scriptures refer to that certainty with a series of extravagant promises which the Lord is pleased to fulfill. These are written to give us a foundation for our pathway of approach to the Lord. This is how God makes a straight path for our feet — to inspire and empower us to come to Him with the right attitude and outlook. His words to us enable us to position ourselves before God in supreme confidence that we are expected and will be received by Him.

> *Grace and peace be multiplied to you in the knowledge of God and of Jesus our Lord; seeing that His divine power has granted to us everything pertaining to life and godliness, through the true knowledge of Him who called us by His own glory and excellence.*
> *For by these He has granted to us His precious and magnificent promises, so that by them you may become partakers of the divine nature, having escaped the corruption that is in the world by lust. [2 Peter 1:2-4]*

Grace and peace are being multiplied to us as we live and move and have our being in Christ. Everything we need to become powerful and godly has been supplied in Christ [Philippians 4:19]. We are called to inherit Jesus, just as He has inherited us from the Father [Ephesians 1:18]. It is His own glory and excellence that is willingly bestowed upon us.

The promises of God are given so that we can fully participate in the nature of Jesus. We share in all that He is and all that He has in Himself. Making us partakers of the divine nature is a wonderful expression of the Father's affection and attitude towards us. It's the evidence of fullness — to be fully like Jesus. We are called to an abundant life, and the sheer size and scale of the promises are designed to convey the wonder of it all.

That we would become as confident in life as the Father is in creation! What would it take for us to live a life of supreme confidence in God — where in His great love for us, we could not fail just simply learn to be better next time; one where the enemy has no power to deceive us because we have left immaturity far behind? We are not children tossed to and fro by lies and false perceptions. We are steadfast, immovable in our trust and assurance of the nature of God to us. Grace surrounds us, peace is increased to us. We are multiplied in the favor of God.

"For the Lord will be your confidence and will keep your foot from being caught." [Proverbs 3:26]

God is very confident in Himself. He seeks to build that confidence into the people He touches with His grace. We can stand before the Lord with the bearing and demeanor of a much loved child in the Presence of a Loving Father.

[1]See my journal on Crafted Prayer at www.brilliantbookhouse.com.

Assignment

- ❊ Examine your current circumstances and describe them.
- ❊ How difficult are they? How do they affect you?

- ❋ What is the provision of God for you in your relationship and experience of Him?
- ❋ What is your upgrade in the Spirit?
- ❋ What favor is God bestowing on you at this time?
- ❋ What will your crafted prayer and declaration look like and sound like as you proclaim it to the problem?

Commission

- ❋ Work through the above exercise then deliberately enter into the problem of a friend and teach them what you have discovered.

Personal Notes

Endurance

Enduring in the face of overwhelming odds is only possible because of the strength of God's grip on us. This is the source of our confidence—we know He will never let us go, no matter what. The will of God is to be for us, as we read in 1 John 5:14-15—

> *Now this is the confidence that we have in Him, that if we ask anything according to His will, He hears us. And if we know that He hears us, whatever we ask, we know that we have the petitions that we have asked of Him.*

With this in mind, we can set our hearts to joyfully endure. The Lord spends a lot of time and effort preparing our hearts to listen to His will. Through this process, we improve our ability to discover His voice, understand His heart, and detect His will. The tipping point in this journey comes when we learn to listen more than speak. When we are in the presence of God, we need to choose our words carefully. *"Do not be rash with your mouth, and let not your heart utter anything hastily before God. For God is in heaven, and you on earth; therefore let your words be few,"* says Ecclesiastes 5:2.

This will sound odd, but I think we sometimes do *too much* praying. If we would simply listen more, we would know exactly what to pray. Instead of using our mouths to try and find God's will, we need to use the ears of our heart. By waiting on God, we will hear His word. We need to remain attentive. Listening is the chief part of prayer.

Prayer is finding out what the Father wants to do, then standing in Christ before Him and asking Him to do it by the power of the Holy Spirit. We pray with God, not towards Him; we pray with the answer, not to try to find one. We are the third part of a three fold chord of answered prayer. Yoked with Jesus in partnership, we rest in God's incredible heart toward us as we joyfully pray His heart back to Him.

When we discover God's will and pray for it to occur, we position ourselves to be part of that answer. We wait, we listen, we determine what to pray, and we pray it—this is how a spiritual warrior works with the Holy Spirit. Prayer is a discipline, preceded by the foundation of listening.

A correct revelation of what the Lord wants to do puts us in the right place at the right time. We then operate with the faith that He hears us, and we know that prayers that reside in the will of God are always answered. Spiritual warriors labor to develop a certainty in prayer so they are not perpetually stuck in petition. As Jesus said in Matthew 21:22, *"Whatever things you ask in prayer, believing, you will receive."* This is the kind of faith with which a spiritual warrior walks. Or as 1 John 5:14-15 puts it—

> *Now this is the confidence that we have in Him, that if we ask anything*

according to His will, He hears us. And
if we know that He hears us, whatever
we ask, we know that we have the
petitions that we have asked of Him.

Prayer is not some massive net we use to trawl for the will of God; it is our opportunity to agree with what He wants to do. When we pray in the will of God, we build the faith and confidence needed to further declare God's plans. Spiritual warriors declare, "This is the will of God," and proclaim the truth of God's victory over every adversary.

A mature Christian moves in thanksgiving and praise even before the answer comes. We translate our prayers into worship and gratitude, pushing the enemy back with our cheerful, declarative faith in God.

When a spiritual warrior combines the will of God with confident prayers, there comes a huge increase of faith. This, in turn, draws God's presence near—He erupts in our heart. Warriors stand their ground confidently and can turn an entire battle with how they pray.

We see this principle in the life of Moses. In Exodus 17, the wandering Israelites battled the Amalekites in Rephidim. Moses stood atop a hill, watching the battle; whenever he lifted his arms in prayer, the Israelites triumphed, as the will of the Lord wanted. When he lowered his arms in fatigue, the battle turned against them. Eventually, others—Aaron and

Hur—came alongside Moses and helped him hold his arms up.

When Moses partnered with the will of God in prayer, the Lord moved. It's not as though the omnipresent God vanished from the battlefield whenever Moses put his arms down—He was still there. But His will was victory over the Amalekites, and He wanted Moses to partner with it. Without that partnership, the Israelites would have lost that fight. Moses did as much fighting by praying as any soldier in the fray did. Confidence, or the lack thereof, can be the difference between breakthrough and defeat.

In Hebrews 10:35-36, we receive a fascinating caution— *"Therefore do not cast away your confidence, which has great reward. For you have need of endurance, so that after you have done the will of God, you may receive the promise."* Too many of us cast away our confidence in the face of adversity. In fact, most Christians toss it overboard as soon as the waves and winds of life stir up.

Spiritual warriors, on the other hand, prize their confidence. They protect it. They let it develop by using it in every circumstance.

I am well known for losing things—keys, wallet, passport, airline tickets. You name it, I've lost it. I have had to make it a habit to check and keep these things with me. It is a conscious, deliberate choice. In the same way, Christians need to make it a habit to check and keep their confidence with them. We have to hold on to our confidence as we would a passport or wallet. In a big city, what's the first thing most men do? We move our wallet from our back pocket to a front one. We want it safe from pickpockets.

We cannot allow the enemy to pickpocket our confidence in Christ. We must not throw it away; we need to keep a firm grip on it at all times. The disciples, in the early days with Jesus, were notorious for abandoning their confidence at every turn. Peter took his eyes off Christ and sank helplessly into the sea. The disciples wondered if a sleeping Jesus even cared that their boat was being battered by a storm. Peter denied even knowing the Lord. Thomas would not accept his best friends' testimony of His resurrection. They constantly squabbled over who would be first in the Kingdom. But these men grew into apostles who led with confidence. Their faith became unshakable, even at the point of death.

The confidence a spiritual warrior carries cannot be pried out of their hands by anything, anytime, anywhere. We are called to hold out for our reward from God, but confidence and endurance must live together within us in order to obtain that reward. Confidence must become our great ally. Endurance must be our best friend.

We are called to be patiently confident and confidently patient. We can hang on in the face of any storm, knowing Jesus is coming. Spiritual warriors are patient people who learn how to silence themselves before God and simply wait for Him to move.

The glue that holds confidence and endurance together is praise. When we choose to praise God for His hand on our life, even when things are rough, we grow quickly. We become stronger than we ever imagined we could be.

We have to fight to receive in warfare. Too many people are willing to give up and just receive whatever they can get; a spiritual warrior contends to get the blessing God has for him. If we throw away our confidence, there is no breakthrough. The enemy knows this better than anyone which is why he constantly works to undermine the confidence of Christians. While most people just want to survive a war, spiritual warriors want to thrive. They want to win, to stand atop the enemy's defeated carcass, and to celebrate. It isn't about being rescued from a tough day. It is about breaking through it into what God has for us.

Warriors love pressure. They want to make the enemy pay for attacking them. They have a special equation: favor plus vengeance equals payback. This breed of warriors have strongly resolved to stand no matter what. They have the tenacity to hold on to the Lord even when everyone else runs away.

Obviously, endurance means no quick victory. Many Christians have been raised on this type of evasion and have no stomach for a war. They are largely event driven. Important spiritual disciplines such as fortitude, persistence, stamina, and perseverance are not part of the vocabulary of many modern churches. We have mostly an escapist theology that means we back down at the intimidation stage or don't even show up for the real fight.

As part of our ongoing training and development, the Lord must, of necessity, allow us to experience life issues that are protracted and not easily solved. That is, He prolongs some situations in order to develop us at a much deeper level. It takes time to go deep; ask any deep sea diver! We simply must have an experience of holding onto the Father through a continual delay as we walk towards eventual resolution. We learn more things about the Father, as well as ourselves. Suffering develops in us a much deeper level of humility and trust. We learn gentleness, forbearance, patience, and steadfastness. There simply is no easy, quick way of developing such powerful disciplines. If we aspire to be real warriors, situations containing the learning about endurance are an absolute necessity.

Real warriors are tough. They know how to endure hardness as good soldiers of Jesus [2 Timothy 2:3]. "If the training is easy, then the player is weak" was the maxim of a rugby coach that I played for in my younger years. There is regular fitness training, and then there is conditioning. The latter means that we put everything into training that he could get out of us. Often we were violently sick. The first month was a nightmare of training, sleeping, and exhaustion. Every muscle ached. It hurt to move; every sinew was protesting. If we did not train at the level demanded, we were off the team. The coach would not commit us to a battle for which we had not properly trained. Rugby is a battle. Forty minutes of mayhem — hard tackling, non-stop running, all action, no time to even catch your breath; a short break at the half, then another forty minutes of grueling, punishing, frequently violent action. I loved it.

We won trophies because we trained properly. In England, anyone can play rugby in the summer months. The weather is nice, the grounds are soft. In winter, when the weather is icy rain, the wind is blowing a gale, the ground is just a sea of mud … that's when fitness tells its own story. The weather conditions will sap the strength right out of you. This is when your conditioning shows through. A tough baseline of conditioning means when everything is against you, only light training is required to maintain fitness. In winter we trained well, but we rested more frequently. We won trophies because we won more games in atrocious conditions. When I meditate on "endure hardness," that's what it means to me. Persist with your training; persevere with a coach who is unrelenting in his capacity to make you properly fit for all the battles ahead.

Our coach never called it "the rugby season"; it was always a campaign — a series of battles to reach a final objective.

So many of the guys with whom I played at that club went on to play professionally and to represent their country at the highest level.

Other teams were afraid to play us, we had the bearing of champions. We were warriors. We expected to win. We had just the right amount of thuggery in the team to compete on any level. Every team needs a few monsters, and we had our fair share — guys who would never quit, men who would run through a brick wall to score a point.

People like Eleazar, one of the three mighty men [monsters!] with David [2 Samuel 23]. Attacked by the Philistines, most of Israel ran. Eleazar fought until his hand was weary and stuck to the sword. That is, his hand gripped the sword with such force, he could not easily unclench it later. He won a great victory and Israel returned in time to plunder the spoils. I want him on my team!

Likewise Shammah, left alone when Israel ran (again!), he defended a patch of lentils and won a great victory. We can rightly think, "Goodness, it's only a patch of lentils." To a warrior though, the fight is the thing, not just the territory. (Unless of course, Shammah planted, watered and cultivated the lentils and planned on eating them! Warriors are funny about such things.) I want him on my team too, along with Josheb, who killed eight hundred soldiers with a spear at one time!

David won and established the kingdom because he had warriors around him, men who knew how to endure. Living in caves, moving around the wilderness, constantly being hounded and pursued by a megalomaniac and his army. Living rough, eating rations, going hungry, never sleeping in the same place for too long — it toughened them up. They learned how to persevere, how to persist in a cause. They were faithful men — loyal to the king, dangerous against the enemy.

Many Christians cannot tell the difference between warfare, adversity, the work of the Cross, and training for reigning. They don't persist; they crumble. An instant society depletes our strength. People are in huge amounts of debt because they cannot wait; they have no patience to save money, then purchase. They mortgage their future to buy trinkets in the present and then declare that God is providing, which may be true. I mean, MasterCard sounds spiritual. A Visa gives you permission to enter, I suppose. Servicing the debt denies us the true flexibility to serve the Lord. We are trapped in the model home that we didn't really need, surrounded by remotes, but with no control over our destiny.

To say yes to Jesus we must also say no to something else. A "yes" is always accompanied by a "no". To be a world class musician, athlete, or actor, it means we have to know what our distractions are going to be and have a plan to overcome them. We have to affirm the need for personal discipline and develop a desire for it. We have to endure hardness, learn to persist when people around us want to give up, cultivate perseverance as a way of life. Ordinary people call it obsession because it suits their own purpose. It's passion — an intense enthusiasm for something, and it requires disciplined pursuit. A focus of intention that mediocre people never attain.

Only people who are strong, solid in their relationship with the Father, firm in the faith, and with an appropriate intensity in the Spirit, can have the potency to force a breakthrough against the odds. Warriors wait for the right opportunity in a battle of wits with the enemy. We have to stay in the fight long enough to see the opportunity in the crisis, and then have sufficient stamina to rise up and grasp it.

Enduring tough times in the right spirit, enables us to combat effectively. Being in tough circumstances for an extended period, without learning or becoming what is required, means that we have waited out the Lord — not waited on Him. We have not produced anything that we can use as a resource, later.

Warriors can sustain others from their own spirit. The qualities produced under pressure will, like a diamond, be of immense value to us and to the situations we encounter in the service of the King. Endurance is about abiding in Christ in such a positive way that His attributes become ours. We literally "put on Christ" [Galatians 3:27]. Until Christ is formed in us, we remain children [Galatians 4:19]. The word children here is "Teknion," which means an infant that has just been weaned off milk.

An army needs soldiers. However, battles are won when soldiers become warriors. Study any military breakthrough in history, and you will discover a warrior at the heart of the conflict. Examine any major breakthrough in science, medicine, or technology; and you will find more people of persistence that kept going when others dropped out. The foothills of Everest are littered with the debris of people who never made the summit.

Is there a warrior in your future? What does your destiny say about your identity? You cannot blame others for not making it. It is your persistence that is required in your life, not theirs. In horseracing, only the first three horses past the post are named. The rest of the field are grouped under the heading "also ran". Thirty horses may compete — twenty seven will be also rans.

Assignment

* In your current circumstances what is your required learning?
* At this time are you reaping something that you sowed in a previous time? What plans do you have to respond, repent, and make restitution?
* What is supposed to be formed of Christ in you, through your present circumstances?

Commission

❊ For what is the Holy Spirit training you?

❊ What prophetic words, dreams, or visions has the Father released in your life?

❊ How do they describe your identity and destiny?

❊ What kind of person must you become in Christ in order for them to be fulfilled?

❊ What strategy are you going to cultivate in order to cooperate with the Holy Spirit in your own development?

Personal Notes

Warriors Break Through for Others

In 2 Samuel 23, we see a prototype of these spiritual warriors in the stories of David's mighty men. Long before he was king, David lived in caves and fought skirmishes against all types of enemies. Along the way, key men joined his cause. Some were mercenaries, others outcasts. Most just loved a good fight. There were thirty ancient superheroes, gladiators who could win any battle. Their stories, handed down through history in Scripture, are awe-inspiring.

Three of them in particular had great renown personally, but joined together to serve a higher cause than their own anointing and prowess.

Adino, Eleazar, and Shammah clearly loved David and feared nothing. All David had to do was dream of something, and these three mighty men went on and made it happen (verses 14-17)—

> *David was then in the stronghold, and the garrison of the Philistines was then in Bethlehem. And David said with longing, "Oh, that someone would give me a drink of the water from the well of Bethlehem, which is by the gate!" So the three mighty men broke through the camp of the Philistines, drew water from the well of Bethlehem that was by the gate, and took it and brought it to David. Nevertheless he would not drink*

it, but poured it out to the LORD. And
he said, "Far be it from me, O LORD,
that I should do this! Is this not the
blood of the men who went in jeopardy
of their lives?" Therefore he would not
drink it.

David had a whim that he wanted to drink from the same well as he did when he was a young boy. Unfortunately, the Philistines controlled that part of the country. Did that stop these mighty men? No! They broke through the line, got the water, and brought it back to their leader. David was so humbled, so awed, by their act that he wouldn't drink it. It was too good for anyone but the Lord Himself.

These three inspired the others to fight on. When warriors join together, they become greater than the sum of their parts. There is a far superior power released through warriors cooperating in the kingdom. Unity releases exponential anointing and power.

Before that can occur, each individual warrior must eventually prove who they are to principalities and powers. Initially we must prove to ourselves also that we belong at this level. The first stage of warfare is concerned with overcoming yourself. We do battle with our flesh when we develop personal disciplines in the Spirit.

"He who is slow to anger is better than the
mighty. And he who rules his spirit, than he
who captures a city." [Proverbs 16:32]

This is why endurance is required. Some breakthroughs take longer than others. A bad habit can take weeks to break and be reformed. We fight two battles over the same issue or problem. The initial battle, to get free; and the second battle, to stay free. The second battle is always to establish the victory of the first encounter. We establish victory when we replace old habits with new ones. We install the new man to replace the old nature. There can be no breakthrough without follow through.

We have all known people who have won the battle to get free, but lost the battle to stay free. The second battle was lost because we did not develop a new life, a new persona, or new disciplines. New never replaced old, which left a vacuum; so the old nature could reassert itself.

Paul said, "In me first." [1 Timothy 1:16] This is a good principle for life in the spirit. There are current breakthroughs that we must receive. To break out of something is the first battle. To break into something is the second. We carry into the corporate warfare the victories we have won personally over ourselves; otherwise we can be a liability in the larger conflict and may even be a door through which the enemy can attack the corporate man.

We see this in the story of Achan, in Joshua chapter 7. There were certain things that the soldiers were not allowed to take as spoil. All the gold, silver, and articles of bronze were to be put into the temple treasury. Achan stole silver and gold and hid it under the floor of his tent.

In Israel's next conflict, which should have been an easy straightforward win over a small village, they were soundly beaten and humiliated. The Lord's assessment was:

> "Israel has sinned, and they have also transgressed My covenant which I commanded them. And they have even taken some of the things under the ban and have both stolen and deceived. Moreover, they have also put them among their own things.
>
> "Therefore the sons of Israel cannot stand before their enemies; they turn their backs before their enemies, for they have become accursed. I will not be with you anymore unless you destroy the things under the ban from your midst.
>
> "Rise up! Consecrate the people and say, 'Consecrate yourselves for tomorrow, for thus the LORD, the God of Israel, has said, "There are things under the ban in your midst, O Israel. You cannot stand before your enemies until you have removed the things under the ban from your midst." [John 7:11-13]

Personal breakthrough cannot occur without an act of repentance and consecration. If we carry deliberate sin into a corporate battle, we will lose the fight. One of the major keys of the kingdom is that we cannot take ground from the enemy if he has ground in us. Sin gives him a legal right over us until we renounce it and are cleansed. The matter with Achan had to be settled before Israel could recapture the anointing of previous conflicts.

In cases of protracted difficulty, when a church is facing ongoing defeat, we may need to call a solemn assembly. This is for the purpose of presenting ourselves to the Lord as a corporate body. As part of the preparation for that each individual must do what is necessary to put things right with God. There is plenty of precedence for this in scripture, notably Nehemiah 9:1-3:

> Now on the twenty-fourth day of this month the sons of Israel assembled with fasting, in sackcloth and with dirt upon them.
> The descendants of Israel separated themselves from all foreigners, and stood and confessed their sins and the iniquities of their fathers.
> While they stood in their place, they read from the book of the law of the LORD their God for a fourth of the day; and for another fourth they confessed and worshiped the LORD their God.

Then some of the key people began to recite the history of the journey of Israel with God from the time of Abram to the present day. This assembly culminated in the writing of a new covenant before the Lord. Chapter 10 details the names of the people who signed it and the conditions that were required from everyone to fulfill it.

In scripture we see that personal sanctification is important for the increase and blessing of the corporate man. The same is true of the family home and business. What blessings are being held up by the enemy because of practiced sin? This is why churches that are judgmental and harsh towards others, seldom grow to the level of their perceived destiny. It is the role of the apostolic and good local leaders to make sure that certain things are not present in the local body. There are several injunctions; here are two which need no further comment:

> *Therefore be imitators of God, as beloved children; and walk in love, just as Christ also loved you and gave Himself up for us, an offering and a sacrifice to God as a fragrant aroma.*
>
> *But immorality or any impurity or greed must not even be named among you, as is proper among saints;*
>
> *and there must be no filthiness and silly talk, or coarse jesting, which are not fitting, but rather giving of thanks.*
>
> *For this you know with certainty, that no immoral or impure person or covetous man, who is an idolater, has an inheritance in the kingdom of Christ and God.*
>
> *Let no one deceive you with empty words, for because of these things the wrath of God comes upon the sons of disobedience.*

Therefore do not be partakers with them.
[Ephesians 5:1-7]

Therefore if you have been raised up with
Christ, keep seeking the things above, where
Christ is, seated at the right hand of God.
Set your mind on the things above, not on the
things that are on earth.

For you have died and your life is hidden with
Christ in God.

When Christ, who is our life, is revealed, then
you also will be revealed with Him in glory.
Therefore consider the members of your earthly
body as dead to immorality, impurity, passion,
evil desire, and greed, which amounts to
idolatry.

For it is because of these things that the wrath
of God will come upon the sons of disobedience,
and in them you also once walked, when you
were living in them.

But now you also, put them all aside: anger,
wrath, malice, slander, and abusive speech from
your mouth.

Do not lie to one another, since you laid aside
the old self with its evil practices,
and have put on the new self who is being
renewed to a true knowledge according to the
image of the One who created him—
a renewal in which there is no distinction
between Greek and Jew, circumcised and

*uncircumcised, barbarian, Scythian, slave and
freeman, but Christ is all, and in all.
So, as those who have been chosen of God, holy
and beloved, put on a heart of compassion,
kindness, humility, gentleness and patience;
bearing with one another, and forgiving each
other, whoever has a complaint against anyone;
just as the Lord forgave you, so also should you.
Beyond all these things put on love, which is
the perfect bond of unity.
Let the peace of Christ rule in your hearts, to
which indeed you were called in one body; and
be thankful.
Let the word of Christ richly dwell within you,
with all wisdom teaching and admonishing one
another with psalms and hymns and spiritual
songs, singing with thankfulness in your hearts
to God.
Whatever you do in word or deed, do all in the
name of the Lord Jesus, giving thanks through
Him to God the Father. [Colossians 3:1-17]*

We are created to destroy the works of the devil
by learning to live in Christ [1 John 3:8]. The enemy has
come to destroy us by stealing our inheritance and
killing our relationships, especially with God [John
10:10]. Who is destroying who in your life? If
abundance is lacking we must ask, what is being
destroyed?

The point of all our development is to produce sons who can glorify God [Hebrews 2:10] and establish the kingdom. Our personal development is vital. There are certain provisions and inheritance that can only come to us on a particular level. There is a level of faithfulness in the spirit where we are entrusted with key revelation and anointing [2 Timothy 2:2]. We are learning to trust the Lord in life and acquiring the capacity to be trusted by Him.

Warriors are breakthrough people. They interrupt the continuity of current events. They disrupt the enemy, and make sure there is a disconnect between him and the local body. They disturb the religious, and mess with traditions that keep people away from encountering the Lord.

Warriors break the power of the enemy in a situation; they render his power inoperative. They create openings for people to upgrade their experience of the Lord Jesus. They crush controlling spirits (whether human or demonic) and set people free to make decisions for themselves. Warriors force entry into a new dimension of the spirit.

The present day church must advance. We must excel in Christ and exceed the early church in signs, wonders, and the Presence of God. People must discover who God really is for them. They must exult in His power over the enemy.

The seventy returned with joy, saying, "Lord, even the demons are subject to us in Your name."

And He said to them, "I was watching Satan fall from heaven like lightning.

"Behold, I have given you authority to tread on serpents and scorpions, and over all the power of the enemy, and nothing will injure you.

"Nevertheless do not rejoice in this, that the spirits are subject to you, but rejoice that your names are recorded in heaven." [Luke 10:17-20]

Warriors love beating the enemy! We need men and women of testimony. People who are proving God joyfully and talking about it. Thankfully there is so much improvement we need to make in order to progress to the place of real power and breakthrough, that We are never going to be short of real opportunities both personally and corporately to destroy the works of the enemy and discover the upgrade that the Father has set aside for us.

We are in a season where we need to reinvent ourselves in the spirit. Call a halt to mediocrity, cast off the role of inferiority, and rise up to occupy the place of promise that is rightfully ours in Christ.

Assignment

❊ What are your current areas of breakthrough that you need to make in life and relationships?

❊ How do you plan to reinvent the parts of your life that are below the level of anointing and fullness that the Father wants you to possess?

Commission

❊ What type of breakthrough does your family, business, ministry, church need at this time?

❊ What is your part in that upgrade?

❊ What particular works of the enemy are you created to destroy?

Personal Notes

Fearlessness

"Let us therefore come boldly to the throne of grace, that we may obtain mercy and find grace to help in time of need," says Hebrews 4:16. Spiritual warriors come boldly to God's throne room, knowing both their own role and His will.

A Christian becomes a spiritual warrior in an instant, singular rite of passage. In that moment, the believer becomes fearless in his approach to God, for he fully understands His nature, fully understands His innate goodness, and fully appreciates the incredible favor He has toward each of us. After that divine encounter we have to develop the discipline, anointing, and faith to stay at this new level and operate from this dimension. We will make mistakes until we fully gain experience in partnering with God's sovereignty. Spiritual warriors know that their capacity to approach God and receive mercy will be a distinguishing feature of their walk in the Spirit. The affection that God has for us cannot be overcome.

We are welcome in God's presence — so welcome, in fact, that the Holy Spirit will help us cut a well-worn path into the presence of God. Grace will overwhelm us again and again—usually when we least deserve it.

Every step we take towards God is an offensive act against the enemy. When we love the Lord God with all of our heart, soul, mind, and strength, we are literally offensive to the enemy. Spiritual warriors know this—when they fall in their humanity and sin, they repent quickly; because even that repentance is an offensive attack on the enemy. A band of warriors says to each other, "The enemy had better kill us, because if all he does is make us stumble, we'll come back even stronger than before." Repentance gives us even more confidence to enter the presence of God, because no penitent soul has ever been turned away by the Holy Spirit. And that boldness in coming to Him inspires others to do the same.

When we combine a supreme confidence in God with our own humility, we are given continuous access to God. Spiritual warriors practice the art of looking into the face of God—always longing to live one more day under His smile. We become preoccupied with His nature, and live a life in His presence.

It is our intimacy that makes us intimidating to the enemy — our confidence in the Father's love, our position in Christ, the fellowship with the Holy Spirit. They all combine in us to take us to a place of being so loved that we lose all fear.

There are many types of fear to which we can give place in our hearts and minds. We know the usual suspects of worry, anxiety, panic, fright, alarm, being apprehensive, nervous, and intimidated.

We can also dread something so much that we turn away from it, no matter the cost. Some people are like that with confrontation. They submit to years of abuse rather than contest a matter. "I didn't like to say anything," is a common comment from the fearful.

When confronted with their own timidity, people will still try to excuse their own acceptance of ill treatment — "It doesn't matter; I've got used to it." Timidity, hesitancy, and shrinking back are all forms of fear that rob us of the pleasure of life and pleasing God [Hebrews 10:38-39].

Not daring something when you have the chance often masks secret fear that has not been dealt with by the Holy Spirit. Believing the worst, expecting something bad — both debilitate us and prevent us from reaching our potential.

Job was a brilliant guy — blameless, upright, fearing God, and turning away from evil [Job 1:1], but in his heart he nurtured a secret fear. He dreaded the fact that one day he might lose everything he possessed. He worried about it constantly, thought of it often. He became tense and nervous at each fluctuation of life. It was growing in him too. Enough for the Father to realize that it was going to become a problem — a self-fulfilling curse. The enemy would be given rights over Job and his family and business because fear is the devil's domain. Fear, unchecked, eventually grows to the point where it torments us [1 John 4:18]. It begins to dominate our conscious mind as well as our unconscious state.

In the end, in order to deliver Job from fear, the Lord had to face him up with it. When it occurs, Job's cry reveals his deepest heart:

> *"For what I fear comes upon me, and what I dread befalls me. "I am not at ease, nor am I quiet, and I am not at rest, but turmoil comes."* *[Job 3:25-26]*

The only antidote to fear is perfect love [1 John 4:18], a love from the Lord that has matured into a place of complete confidence. Mature love has a settled nature to it that cannot be overcome. This is the root of fearlessness. If we know with absolute certainty that we are accepted and loved, we are not afraid to make mistakes. We try things knowing that we are covered. In any contest, we cannot win if we are afraid to lose.

Hesitancy and timidity are shackles that bind us just as surely as horror and dread. Fear of man prevents us from stepping out in faith. The biggest fear in the prophetic realm that prevents people from speaking, is the fear of being wrong. The biggest fear in giving a word of knowledge concerning sickness is our not having the faith in God to back it up.

We forget sometimes that the Father is a believer too! He loves to believe in us. He has faith in His own abilities in and through us.

When He gives us a word of knowledge, His own faith is on the line, together with ours, to back us up and empower us to succeed.

Fearless people give courage. We inspire people to believe. We influence people to trust in the Lord. We infuse faith into people. In the modern ear Bill Johnson and Randy Clark are brilliant at this. I remember when Randy took a small team of friends to be with him in Philadelphia the year he first began to do his own crusades. We slept in a room in the church for about eight days together — in the bunker, we called it — just to be an encouragement to him. His first talk was, "God can use little ol' me." Inspired by him, we all moved out of our comfort zone to move in the supernatural (though not as much as Randy!) He was so determined to occupy that place of promise. His fearlessness has increased considerably. When you meet the people that Randy has trained and mentored, they have that same quality of astonishing simple trust in the bigness of God.

Spiritual warriors give courage to people. They are refreshing to be around. They have that sense of being indomitable, impossible to subdue. Soldiers line up behind warriors because they know there is an excellent chance of victory. Warriors make things happen. Good people add something to us by who they are and how they live. Other people are negative and take things away; still others have a contrary spirit and become divisive. Warriors multiply. They give more than is required. Measure has no meaning for them. Abundance is their language and way of life. When you meet real warriors they overwhelm you with possibilities and refresh you with their certainties.

They are unafraid, and it shows. They attract faith and power. It's in their mindset, their attitude, their bearing. They wear it like armor. They contribute these things to the atmosphere around them. They create a better environment because they are massively in league with the Creator. They help to shape the way we position ourselves to fight in the situation we are facing. Such warriors have heard the Lord laughing at the enemy. It echoes in their own hearts. They feed off the sound of victory.

We train for this position, using our lifestyle situations. We learn the craft of obedience and submission to the great heart of God. As He is, so are we in this world. Heaven coming to earth in our own hearts. What a glorious way to live. Far above all principalities and powers — no longer earthbound, but seated with Christ in heavenly places [Ephesians 1:18-23 and 2:4-10]. Living a life that exemplifies a revelatory understanding of our place and position in Christ — being partakers of a level of kindness unheard of on the earth.

A God's lovingkindness, so huge it reduces every opposing force and idea to a ridiculous minimum. Warriors love freedom and are fierce about it. It is for freedom that Christ has set us free. We are partners with Christ in releasing people from captivity. Warriors do not imprison people; they bind the enemy. They cast out devils. It is their fearless nature that we need to relish and respect.

Jesus is a warrior. He is the King and champion of our hearts. Fearlessness is the norm; anything less is merely bravado.

Assignment

* Be honest about your current tensions, fears, and apprehensions.
* What would be the opposite of them that you need to ask the Holy Spirit to give you? Make a list of these characteristics.
* Apply them to the situation you are in. Cultivate the mind and persona that creates space for this attribute to overpower your circumstances.

Commission

* If you wanted someone to write a eulogy about you being a warrior, what would you want them to say? Write one out for yourself.
* What would have to change in you to make that eulogy become the truth?

Personal Notes

A Revelatory Capacity to Receive

If our spirituality matters, it matters most under pressure. The Lord is with us always; he never leaves nor forsakes us [Hebrews 13:5]. He is our rock, an ever-present help in times of trouble [Psalm 27:5]. He lifts us up above our enemies [Psalm 27:6]. He sustains us. His willingness to help us is the foundation of our relationship with Him.

> *'Do not fear, for I am with you;*
> *Do not anxiously look about you, for I am your God.*
> *I will strengthen you, surely I will help you,*
> *Surely I will uphold you with My righteous right hand.' [Isaiah 41:10]*

When we dwell on our circumstances, we become circumstantial. That is, we are drawn up in all of the tiny details of the situation. We attempt, spiritually, to bring God into our circumstances. We pray to Him through the details of the situation, often telling Him the things He already knows — like He is the child, and we are the parent — explaining everything. We try to develop peace in the situation. We attempt joy, but it mostly feels false and is intended to impress others.

We do not live in our circumstances, we live in Christ. Our capacity to receive depends upon our position. We can sit in the circumstances or be seated in

Christ in heavenly places. We cannot do both; so a choice is required.

When the Father draws us to Him, He seeks to separate us from our circumstances. That is why He tells us to come away into our prayer closet [Matthew 6:6]. We come into a confined space where we can confide in Him. A closet is a restricted place where we are shut in with God and the enemy is restrained. We do not take our problems into the closet; we take our beliefs, our childlike simplicity, our uncomplicated trust. We come to worship and adore — to get into the face of Father and relax.

We need His strength in order to prosper. His nature is so inspirational; it strengthens us immeasurably. His delight is contagious, His joy unbounded. His peace is a deep, rhythmic rest that renews our mind. We feel lighthearted in His Presence. We joyfully cast all our cares onto Him.

In times of incredible assault, adversity, and pressure, I have entered my secret place and become so confined with the Lord I forgot my reason for entry. I have discovered later that the enemy has got tired of waiting around (he has no access to patience; it's impossible for him) and decamped.

Allow the Father to separate you from your circumstances. Cast your cares on Him; then come away with Him. Let the Holy Spirit take you upwards to the Father. You are in Christ — you can go anywhere! In the place of intimate affection you receive a revelatory perspective that empowers you to be resourced from Heaven.

On earth a crisis is perceived as a threat to our well being. In Heaven it is an opportunity to discover something. The turning point for us is being confined with God — being in a space that He fully occupies. He surrounds us, fills us, overwhelms us. We are astonished, mesmerized. He lets us look through His eyes, feel His heartbeat. Joy becomes unconfined in that small space. We rejoice because His viewpoint is so amazing that we want to rush out of heaven into our circumstances and live out what we are seeing.

There is no crisis of belief in intimacy, there is the certainty of faith; "I know whom I have believed and I am persuaded that He is able to keep what I have entrusted to Him" [2 Timothy 1:12].

The keys of the Kingdom are given to people of revelatory insight. "Blessed are you Simon, because flesh and blood did not reveal this to you. It was My Father in Heaven." [Matthew 16:17] The keys to bind and lose come to us from our heavenly space. The place of revelation is within, where Christ dwells. It's not available to a casual seeker but always opens to a worshipper.

Joy, praise, rejoicing, and thanksgiving are all forms of a celebratory lifestyle that make it easier to enter the secret place in times of difficulty. Warriors practice being at rest. It is customary for them to spend excess time in worship. Rejoicing is their breath — a joyful, simple lifting of the heart in praise.

In times of great trial and stress I have become so grateful to the Father for the gift of speaking in tongues. How wonderful to transcend thought and logic! How amazing not to be earthbound. The gift of a heavenly language takes us up and away from our circumstances. Tongues comes straight out of our innermost being, our deepest heart, and touches God so quickly. We are transported into another dimension. It's almost like time traveling. We close our eyes and speak in tongues out loud. As we continue, the world drops away from us, and we enter a different dimension of God's Presence.

Speaking in tongues has no reason attached to it, only a heaven-sent intuition. No wonder Paul exclaimed, "I speak in tongues more than you all." When we examine the wonderful revelations of Christ he received, it would make us want to speak in tongues also! When we examine his marvelous insights on life in the Spirit and his deep adoration of Jesus, we know why He spent extra time using his heavenly language. It's a transport device. It takes us directly into God's Presence; "We come boldly before the throne of grace." What a fabulous gift!

I have several languages in the Spirit. My intimate language sounds vaguely Italian; all I know is it soothes my heart to adore God this way. A great peace fills me. Often I have felt an astonishing lightness come over me. Every ounce of stress and tension melts away. The experience can be so powerful that I have to wait for strength to return to my body so that I can move again. During this time I can see a vision of my circumstances only with a different ending. I get to see what I should say and do. Revelatory keys come to me that open up the situation in a way that I would not have imagined.

My First Nation friends in America have often told me that they hear parts of their own language in my warfare tongue. Sioux, Cheyenne, Navajo, Apache, and Cherokee; to name a few. For me it is the language of declaration to God. When I speak out in this purpose, my voice is soft, distinctive. My heart is full of who God is, and I have to declare His goodness and beauty, power and sovereignty.

When I move into proclamation over the enemy or particular circumstances, my voice changes. My spirit rises up; strength fills me. My eyes flash. A confidence swells up in my chest. These are fighting words. The enemy often disappears at this point. Maybe he hears something in the sound of the voice. He is vulnerable to God's power, that we know.

Speaking in tongues is a revelatory language that opens us up to the claims of heaven in our circumstances. I love my everyday language too. Just to be able to quite naturally lift my heart to God and pour out words that are heartfelt, not logic-driven, is such a beautiful experience.

Spiritual warriors are lovers of God. We can't let a day go by without expressing our love, adoration, and desire for the Lord. We are love-sick people who just want to live one more day under His smile. We are occupied with Him, and the confidence He gives us empowers us to see life through His lens.

The Father's lens is always Jesus. He put us into Christ so that He could always see us in and through His Beloved Son. We are accepted in the Beloved [Ephesians 1:6]. We have a revelatory language that aids perception and releases provision.

There is no doubt in my own mind that speaking in tongues has empowered me, more than any other gift, to stand still and see the salvation of the Lord. It enables me to have a heart relationship with God that refreshes my soul, renews my mind, and increases my faith. Speaking in tongues is a gift that seldom comes alone. It travels with wisdom, the word of knowledge, and prophecy. They are all revelatory insights: 100% military intelligence that is real and accurate, beforehand knowledge of the plans of the enemy [2 Kings 6:8-12]. Prophecy is history, spoke in advance — the future opening up to the present. Wisdom is the ability to know how God thinks, how He perceives, and how He likes to do things.

Beloved, this is not a fair fight. The weapons of our warfare are divinely inspired and powerful against enemy strongholds [2 Corinthians 10:4]. To receive under pressure is our privilege. The Holy Spirit replaces the tyranny of the enemy with the peace of God that passes all understanding. There is no logic to it; it's beyond that completely. Logic keeps us earthbound. Revelatory insight comes from a different dimension. It is a manifestation of the Spirit that comes from being in Christ in heavenly places.

Speaking in tongues is not an option, but a necessity. We can all speak in tongues; it is the language of heaven. Only logic prevents its reception and use. If you do not speak in tongues, ask the Holy Spirit for the gift. It is your right and privilege.

Speak out of your heart, not your head. The Holy Spirit uses our will and emotions first. Our mind is influenced by our Spirit, and we receive a renewed capacity to think differently [Ephesians 4:20-24]. Our former manner of life was logical and reasonable. Our new man is intuitive, revelatory, and spiritual. What we hear in our spirit reforms our thinking. God does not speak to intellect; but He does use it, eventually. He communicates to our heart. The inner man of the spirit hears His voice. His words rise up in our hearts to touch our mind.

When He speaks to our hearts we have an experience of Him to go with His words. If we try to receive Him in our head first, logic will make experience redundant. It is possible to have knowledge without wisdom. We know much, but we have no experience of what we know. Eventually we are disinherited because we know about God, but we don't know Him. We are like the elder brother who remained with the Father, but knew Him less than the prodigal.

This is the land of the religious and the Pharisee, where men make God in their own image; and intellectual study governs our thinking. We have no internal perception of God's true reality, and our logic-based faith is so reasonable we cannot achieve anything with it.

Assignment

- ❊ If you do not yet speak in tongues, you must ask for the gift. You need it; God wants you to have it. That settles it.
- ❊ Ask and you will receive. Keep on asking. That's the joy of prayer — certain communication that yields brilliant results.
- ❊ When you feel ready in your heart, open your mouth and speak out loud. (It's an emotion. You'll love it!)
- ❊ It's a language like any other. It has structure, intonation. It may sound like one you know or have heard — that's OK.
- ❊ HAVE FUN!! Enjoy the experience. Language develops — ask any three-year-old.

Commission

❃ Get into a stronger habit of speaking in tongues more.

❃ Ask for a second language or a third. Each language needs a particular purpose, so pay attention to how you are going to use it.

❃ Remember: speak out loud. Feel the emotion of it. Relax in the intuition it brings.

❃ Have a notebook handy. Ask the Holy Spirit for an interpretation of what you prayed or declared. Don't use reason when you listen (that comes later). Use intuition. Write down what you feel.

❃ Meditate on that. Think deeply. Keep a journal. Enjoy life.

Personal Notes

Preoccupied with Jesus

The LORD bless you, and keep you;
The LORD make His face shine on you,
And be gracious to you;
The LORD lift up His countenance on you,
And give you peace.'
[Numbers 6:24-26]

What a wonderful, poetic expression: "The Lord make His face shine upon you." That's the best description of a smile that I have ever encountered. Everything about God sparkles to me. His glory glistens with happiness. He shimmers with delight. His eyes twinkle with goodness. He bubbles in enthusiasm for us.

He has this wonderful beam in His face when He looks at us. A glint in His eye, a glow in His smile. His voice is brilliant, dazzling in its beauty. It captivates us. The Father has this astonishing gaiety and vitality. Full of life and spirit. He is radiant. His face shines upon us!

There is a luster in the way He communes with us; a brilliant, glorious, luminescence that captures our affection and makes us feel what He feels. His heartbeat is enchanting. There have been many times when I have been so overwhelmed by His Presence, that I cannot decide what to do in my pleasure. Do I cry with happiness? Do I sing aloud for joy? Do I sit, silent and astonished? Do I do all three? Do I dance wildly, shout

out praises, or just look at Him in awe? That's why the song "I Can Only Imagine" by Mercy Me is so powerful to me. They are singing my experience of God.

My heart bubbles over with the memory of His abundant goodness [Psalm 145:7]. He is righteous in all His ways and kind in all His deeds [Psalm 145:17]. Being occupied with Him is delightful. He chooses very carefully the chief revelation He wants you to possess about His nature. All subsequent revelation will flow out of this one truth that will underpin every experience of God you will ever have in this life. This truth is a major party of your inheritance word. It will cause you to receive in every area of your life, no matter what is against you. For me, it is the kindness of God. He is the kindest person I have ever known. His lovingkindness has overwhelmed my heart and my life now for many, many years. It has changed my character. It has upgraded my personality. It has radically altered my behavior.

Lovingkindness is my own personal highway into the Presence of the Lord. It dominates my thinking; overrules my perceptions; and maintains my heart in a place of joy, warmth, and rest. In late 1989, the Lord first began talking to me about lovingkindness becoming my sure, certain way into His Presence. Since then the Holy Spirit has consistently and relentlessly pursued me with this revelation. At the time of writing, more than 6,700 days have passed since I began this journey into kindness.

I cannot remember a day in that timeframe when He did not say or do something out of His lovingkindness to me. During that time I went through some horrendous experiences of life where only the revelation and experience of lovingkindness kept me safe and in my right mind. At times the negativity surrounding me was so pronounced it could have been devastating, I found out who were my real friends. Relationships around me were pruned to a minimum by an enemy committed to my destruction. It was a time of desolation where the spoiler ransacked my life, and I lost everything that had been built.

Relentlessly, day after day, the Holy Spirit showed up with immense comfort, deep joy, and rest — pure, sweet rest. I felt my anger leave. Resentment and bitterness were reduced so radically, I misplaced them for months at a time. When they returned on days, I just smiled and refused. I kept my own counsel (and still do) about those days. The Lord has conquered my thoughts with much better ones, right out of His heart. Everyday He taught me how to see people and events His way. He touched my heart constantly. In the early days I was a poor student, but His endless patience and lovingkindness wore down my flesh until it died — overwhelmed by grace.

He showed me myself and then proceeded to love me so outrageously that it broke my heart. I was worse than anyone I knew; and He touched me, kissed me, loved on me until I capitulated. Whatever God is,

He is relentless. He never quits. There would be times when I would get angry with His goodness towards me. I wanted a pity party. I wanted to vindicate myself to my detractors. I wanted to be right! I wanted to show them a thing or two. I did not want to be just good to them.

Slowly, I realized that if God granted that desire, all I could reveal would be my flesh. I would be confirming their worst suspicions. It's a hard place to be in — when you have not done what you are accused of; but if you get angry and speak out of that, — you reveal in defense what they are attacking you for in the first place!

I began to learn about being preoccupied with Jesus. I learned to understand that if I defended myself, what self was I defending? I became silent towards people and vocal towards God. I discovered a wonderful thing — how to die quietly! The enemy wants hatred to have a voice. Bitterness and resentment, when verbalized, become more entrenched.

In the lovingkindness of God, I let it all go. There is a lot to be said in favor of dumbness [Isaiah 53:7]. The enemy leaves much more quickly when we refuse to rage. Silence oppresses him. Rest infuriates him. The cross debilitates him. the Holy Spirit was marvelous to me all that time — relentless in His patience, unending in His enthusiasm for me. Gradually my head broke above the surface. I moved on, found new people, began to develop new friends. I learned the same lessons again but at a deeper level. I began to see that some friendships were offered, but the price was too high. It was love with a hook — people giving, but wanting in return things I could not give.

The difference in me was profound. I had the freedom to see that I could play a small part in someone's life but not be responsible for the whole — just the piece. I stopped trying to fix things and just lovingly gave my one or two pieces. When the Spirit was ready, He moved me along. I have great, new friends. I am learning the piece that I get to be for them. The whole is God's responsibility.

I love putting relentless and kindness together in the same sentence. God has been relentlessly kind to me. Now I know no other way to live, think, or speak. I'm not perfect in it, but I am much more mature than I was.

The initial revelation that the Father gives us becomes our main point of growth, development, and adjustment. My advice to people that I am discipling is for them to choose an aspect of God's nature and character that they are fully attracted to and begin to develop, with the Holy Spirit, a lifestyle commensurate with that truth. Our thinking, speaking, seeing, and behaving all arrange themselves behind and within that truth.

Each day then becomes a lesson in alignment — a choosing to cultivate that lifestyle. The Holy Spirit is astonishingly brilliant at this type of development. He excels as teacher and facilitator. He has not come to teach us all truth, but to lead us into all truth. He teaches, then creates the scenario in which we can experience the truth by putting it into practice.

This is how we become preoccupied with Jesus — through ongoing development. It is vital that this is not a chore, but a delight.

All revelation of God must result in us seeing His glory and being dazzled by His radiance. Our relationship with God is always extrovert. No matter our personality type, we are called at some point to shout, sing aloud, rejoice, dance, and declare enthusiastically who He is for us. Worship has a loud voice. I'm an introvert. I love my personality. I like the way the Father made me. I'm a deep thinker, and I adore wisdom. Joy has no introversion. It is exuberant, ardent, earnest, excited, fervent, hearty, lively, wholehearted, and zealous. It is passionate, vehement, and fanatical in it's appreciation, value, and impression of God.

So if you're like me, you'll have to get over yourself. It may help you to know that extroverts also struggle with their personality. Patience, rest, and wisdom are not easily won by extroverts. The point is, we must develop our relationship with God across the extremes of personality. Initially its tough, eventually it's fun. The Father did not make me to be an introvert only. He made me to be an introvert with joyful, passionate, exuberant intimacy.

All that brilliance of God rubs off on us, and we move into a more rounded expression of ourselves. Joy in the Lord has changed me. I have become more outgoing — more of a story teller and have developed a couple of stand up comedy routines. (No, I do not take bookings —thanks for asking!) Being preoccupied with Jesus brings a deep enjoyment of life in all its shades. We live each day under God's smile. We do the things that bring Him pleasure. We bask in the warmth of His affection. We cooperate with a generous Holy Spirit who reveals Jesus to us. We fall more under the spell of this radical Savior who fills us with Himself. We learn His pleasures and develop them to please Him. Every circumstance is His opportunity to shine over us and to us. In our preoccupation, we become God-conscious. Pleasure, delight, warmth, and happiness become conspicuous. The Father is jubilant about Jesus and therefore overjoyed with us in all our learning and becoming.

The Holy Spirit is so immensely cheerful and thrilled about revealing Jesus to us. Our fellowship is wrapped in gladness and enjoyment. This is the Good News, and we are living it and loving it!

Assignment

❊ Ask the Holy Spirit to give you one aspect of God's nature that He most wants to make your biggest spiritual experience. It could be the self ⁻

revelation of God in Exodus 34:6-7; one of the fruits of the Spirit in Galatians 5; mercy, delight, or majesty.

❋ Learn to see, think, and experience everything in life by this attribute — through this aspect of God's nature.

❋ You must be faithful to God's nature above all things.

Commission

❋ Using this aspect of God's nature, develop a worship theme for your own life. Write crafted psalms of thanksgiving, rejoicing, and praise around God's revelation of Himself.

❋ Let the Holy Spirit be relentless to you. Live in this truth deliberately, consciously — until it lives in you radically.

❋ Keep a journal, a record of your journey. Chronicle your experience and how you overcame the enemy by being overjoyed in the Lord.

Personal Notes

Understanding Crisis and Process

God seeks the pleasure of our company, and He wants us to live in that place forever. Spiritual warriors know that every situation has been designed for us to discover God's Presence and find appropriate access, using our circumstances.

Confidence in His nature is our entry point, always. To live in His Presence with confidence is His will for us. Our inheritance is to belong to the Presence of God with utter conviction and assurance.

The word "warrior" conjures up images of violence and conflict, confrontation and opposition. While there is obviously some truth in that (we are called to fight) a warrior is so much more than that. The weapons of our warfare are more powerful than the ones the enemy wants to use on us. A spiritual warrior is essentially peaceful, untroubled, and calm. That place of calm and tranquility is the source of internal power and anointing that causes God's people to overcome.

We win through peace! We overcome by being overjoyed. We overthrow by being overwhelmed. The goodness of God, the sheer beauty of His nature, has so captivated and filled us that the enemy is pushed away and given no room in our lives. All our permissions are given by God. We want Him to affect and influence us. Opposition attaches to what we don't remove. We have reclaimed our inner territory so that we can recover the ground around us.

A spiritual warrior has many positive attributes of dedication, focus, commitment, and discipline. These are all earthed in a joy that is contagious and a peace that is outrageous. They have been overwhelmed by love, and it shows. They have an exuberance in grace that wins people to the truth of God.

Warriors have a clarity of vision plus the internal compass and resources to keep going in that direction, no matter what is happening or how powerful the opposition is against them. Under real pressure, we fold; or we focus.

Every champion in scripture seemed to move from one crisis to another. Warriors know that there can be no crisis without process. Process is a series of steps that take us from one place to another. Process is where the Father reveals His intentionality, His purpose, His plan. No matter how powerful the opposition is, God has a plan for them.

Pharaoh, the most despotic ruler on the planet in the time of the ascendancy of Egypt, had to learn his place in the purpose of God.

> *And the LORD hardened Pharaoh's heart, and he did not listen to them, just as the LORD had spoken to Moses.*
> *Then the LORD said to Moses, "Rise up early in the morning and stand before Pharaoh and say to him, 'Thus says the LORD, the God of the Hebrews, "Let My people go, that they may serve Me.*

"For this time I will send all My plagues on you and your servants and your people, so that you may know that there is no one like Me in all the earth.

"For if by now I had put forth My hand and struck you and your people with pestilence, you would then have been cut off from the earth.

"But, indeed, for this reason I have allowed you to remain, in order to show you My power and in order to proclaim My name through all the earth.

"Still you exalt yourself against My people by not letting them go.

[Exodus 9:12-17]

For the Scripture says to Pharaoh, "ᵃFOR THIS VERY PURPOSE I RAISED YOU UP, TO DEMONSTRATE MY POWER IN YOU, AND THAT MY NAME MIGHT BE PROCLAIMED THROUGHOUT THE WHOLE EARTH." [Romans 9:17]

God hardened Pharaoh's heart so that he resisted against Moses. The Lord is in charge of our opposition for His own purpose. Our role is to cooperate with the Sovereignty of God. Many times on the mission field I came up against human opposition in the face of petty, power — hungry officialdom. We never got angry or felt helpless. Often we just waited and prayed. We chose not to be desperate, but calm. We got into the face of God for our confirmation; we never believed man. Doors would open because God was with us. Sometimes it would be dramatic; most times we didn't know what happened.

In the old Soviet bloc, crossing into what was then East Germany, we were held up at the border. Our vehicle was pulled out of line, and we were slammed up against the blockhouse wall guarded by some very zealous KGB officials. Our papers were taken away to another building a hundred meters away. For anyone who traveled in Communist countries this was a normal experience for Westerners. We quietly spoke in tongues. It's important that we are calm, ordinary.

Often we were interrogated — sometimes roughly, occasionally with brutality. Peace is important. In that regime, fear is evidence of guilt. Sometimes we met soldiers who were bored, looking for some sport. If they detected fear, they would beat a confession out of people. Rest is a weapon.

On this occasion, our guards suddenly lost interest in us and walked away. A soldier came out of the building we were leaning against and gave us our papers. We looked at the building down the road where our papers had been taken, smiled, shrugged our shoulders, and drove across the border, carrying two hundred bibles in our luggage.

Pharaoh had his purpose; so did Moses. There is no one like God in all the earth. We have to learn that, and so does the evil one. The Lord loves to show His power to the enemy. Our role in His majesty is to proclaim Him. That's what David did against Goliath.

Proclamation intimidates; that's why we do it. We fight the good fight [1 Timothy 6:12] of faith. A good fight is one that we don't lose.

Crisis is a normal event on the road to fulfilling our destiny:

> *"but in everything commending ourselves as*
> *servants of God, in much endurance, in*
> *afflictions, in hardships, in distresses,*
> *in beatings, in imprisonments, in tumults, in*
> *labors, in sleeplessness, in hunger,*
> *in purity, in knowledge, in patience, in*
> *kindness, in the Holy Spirit, in genuine love,*
> *in the word of truth, in the power of God; by*
> *the weapons of righteousness for the right hand*
> *and the left,*
> *by glory and dishonor, by evil report and good*
> *report; regarded as deceivers and yet true;*
> *as unknown yet well-known, as dying yet*
> *behold, we live; as punished yet not put to*
> *death,*
> *as sorrowful yet always rejoicing, as poor yet*
> *making many rich, as having nothing yet*
> *possessing all things. [2 Corinthians 6:4-10]*
> *Are they servants of Christ?—I speak as if*
> *insane—I more so; in far more labors, in far*
> *more imprisonments, beaten times without*
> *number, often in danger of death.*
> *Five times I received from the Jews thirty-nine*
> *lashes.*

Three times I was beaten with rods, once I was
stoned, three times I was shipwrecked, a night
and a day I have spent in the deep.
I have been on frequent journeys, in dangers
from rivers, dangers from robbers, dangers from
my countrymen, dangers from the Gentiles,
dangers in the city, dangers in the wilderness,
dangers on the sea, dangers among false
brethren;
I have been in labor and hardship, through
many sleepless nights, in hunger and thirst,
often without food, in cold and exposure.
Apart from such external things, there is the
daily pressure on me of concern for all the
churches.
Who is weak without my being weak? Who is
led into sin without my intense concern?
If I have to boast, I will boast of what pertains to
my weakness.
[2 Corinthians 11:23-30]

Paul experienced highs and lows in life and circumstances. He knew that he would always have favor with God even when there was no favor with man. Whenever I was beaten on the mission field, I never attributed that to disfavor with God. Sometimes the favor of God lies in what could have happened but didn't, as well as in what did happen that was better than we imagined. A true warrior has already given their life away. It does not belong to them but to Christ.
his

"For me to live is Christ, to die is gain," [Philippians 1:21] was Paul's battle cry (among others). He had a fine sense of himself in the worth and value of Jesus. He had suffered the loss of all things and counted that as a minimal thing compared to knowing Jesus [Philippians 3:8]. He knew that there are times when a warrior puts the life of Christ on the line for the purposes of God [Philippians 3:10]. We are not putting our lives on the line. "We are dead and our lives are hid with Christ in God' [Colossians 3:3].

Christ is our life [Colossians 3:4]; and when He is revealed in us, His glory is manifested also. Warriors, when confronted with a huge challenge or an assault, do not immediately march out to deal with the enemy. Rather, they first march into their innermost being to submit to God. Maturity in our inner man is the key to remaining in tune with God on the battlefield.

They march inwardly to be changed; they march outwardly to make a change. That inner place is our refuge in God that also becomes a fortress against the enemy. A safe place in God becomes a strong place against the enemy. What we have in God we hold over the enemy.

This internal space where our inner man is constantly in fellowship with Christ within, provides us with the ability to look at the invisible realm of the kingdom. When we view life in the Spirit from this place it is impossible to be downhearted. We see through the eyes of an ever-present Christ. His perspective on life is glorious.

> *Therefore we do not lose heart, but though our outer man is decaying, yet our inner man is being renewed day by day.*
> *For momentary, light affliction is producing for us an eternal weight of glory far beyond all comparison,*
> *while we look not at the things which are seen, but at the things which are not seen; for the things which are seen are temporal, but the things which are not seen are eternal. [2 Corinthians 4:16-18]*

When Christ controls our inner space, His glory is manifested within. The kingdom opens up all the possibilities of heaven to us. The invisible becomes as real to us as the temporal. The spiritual dimension of Christ within becomes more real for us than the natural realm. We have reached our seat of government. In this place, all powers of the enemy, assaults, difficulties, problems, and adversity become downgraded to a "light and momentary affliction." What a brilliant concept! Its an astonishing point of view. Christ within — the confident expectation of glory [Colossians 1:27]. What was Paul seeing in his spirit that made him downgrade the enemy and adversity to such a ridiculous level? It was that these outward problems paled in comparison to the rich inward life of the King and His Kingdom.

The Old Covenant heroes proved these truths about the Presence of God, and they did not have Christ within. Daniel knew God so well; he was described by an angel as a man "greatly beloved" of God. Daniel was a force for good and for God from within the very heart of the Babylonian and Persian empires. He served several world rulers, notably Nebuchadnezzar of Babylon and Cyrus of Persia. Daniel's story is a testimony to how God works in us and through us no matter how difficult our surroundings.

Daniel was one of three governors overseeing 120 regional officers who wielded great power in the provinces. The king was so impressed by the excellent spirit in Daniel, he gave thought to promoting him over the whole realm. The other powers in the land were horrified at this and conspired against Daniel. They could find no fault in his faithful stewardship of Darius the king, but they discovered an opportunity against Daniel through his relationship with God. Daniel loved to pray three times a day. They knew that Daniel faithfully obeyed the law of the land; but when that law conflicted with the law of God, Daniel would choose the latter.

They convinced the king to write a decree stating that no one could pray for thirty days. If they broke this law they would be thrown into a lions' dens. Once a royal decree was made, it could not be revoked until its time of expiration. Daniel is thrown into the lions' den, has an angelic visitation [Daniel 6:21-22],

and is miraculously delivered. The king is so
overwhelmed he writes a decree:

> *Then Darius the king wrote to all the peoples,*
> *nations and men of every language who were*
> *living in all the land: "May your peace abound!*
> *"I make a decree that in all the dominion of my*
> *kingdom men are to fear and tremble before the*
> *God of Daniel;*
> *For He is the living God and enduring forever,*
> *And His kingdom is one which will not be*
> *destroyed,*
> *And His dominion will be forever.*
> *"He delivers and rescues and performs signs and*
> *wonders*
> *In heaven and on earth,*
> *Who has also delivered Daniel from the*
> *power of the lions."*
> *So this Daniel enjoyed success in the reign of*
> *Darius and in the reign of Cyrus the Persian.*
> *[Daniel 6:25-28]*

Daniel also had three friends: Shadrach,
Meshach, and Abed-Nego who faced a similar problem
of jealously, lies, power-broking, and corruption in the
time of Nebuchadnezzar [Daniel chapter 3]. The king
made a golden image and ordered that everyone should
attend its dedication ceremony and bow down before it.
Daniel's friends refused to obey the command and were
brought before the king who was furious with them.
They knew the penalty for disobedience. They knew

the options available to them — bow down or die a horrible death.

They answered the king immediately [Daniel 3:16-18]:

> *Shadrach, Meshach and Abed-nego replied to the king, "O Nebuchadnezzar, we do not need to give you an answer concerning this matter. "If it be so, our God whom we serve is able to deliver us from the furnace of blazing fire; and He will deliver us out of your hand, O king. "But even if He does not, let it be known to you, O king, that we are not going to serve your gods or worship the golden image that you have set up."*

This is a predetermined response, composed in advance. Warriors are always clear in their thinking and their responses. The king was so outraged he had a furnace heated seven times hotter than normal. The soldiers who threw them into the furnace were killed by the flames. The king was astonished to see four men in the furnace, not three; and the fourth was unlike anyone he had ever seen [3:25]. Everyone was amazed and astounded that Shadrach, Meshach, and Abed-Nego were not only alive; they had not one burn, their clothing was intact, and there was no smell of smoke on their bodies! Nebuchadnezzar also passed a decree that no one could speak against the God of the Hebrews. He promoted the men to serve as governors in the province of Babylon.

Champions have a view of God that sets them apart in their day. They understand that all crises are part of a process that God has set in motion. They are not overwhelmed by the event because they are aware of the process that God is developing around them to train, equip, and empower them in His name.

The process is always about our development into the place that the Father has set aside for us in Christ. Through all the ups and downs of our life's journey, when we commit ourselves to the process of God, we grow up in all things in Christ. Immature people only focus on the crisis itself, not the bigger picture of their own development. The Father gives us prophecy so that we can get a handle on our identity for the future. All our life circumstances after that are designed to produce the character, quality, personality, and attitude that we need to develop in order to become the person He envisages us to be in Christ.

Process is where we discover God at work in our lives. It is where we submit to the work of His hands. Process is everything. There is no growth or maturity without it. If we do not submit to the process, the enemy will not submit to us. The process is the foundation for our obedience which results in our authority. There is no authority outside of our submission.

Process is joyful. It's full of learning and love and Presence. Process is Discipleship 101 with the Holy

Spirit. We are personally mentored in life by the third member of the Trinity! Yahoo, and again I say, yahoo!!

The Holy Spirit is breathtakingly brilliant. The best teacher, facilitator, and mentor — absolutely fabulous! He loves to lead us into experiences of truth. He is so amazingly wise about everything — a genius, in fact. And, most astonishingly He is our Comforter on the days when the lessons are really tough. Warriors must have tough training at times to acclimate them to places of real power and strength. We learn obedience by the things that we suffer [Hebrews 5:8]. In saying "yes" to Jesus, we must say "no" to other people and other things. Sometimes the "no" is painful.

The process that the Father seeks to commit us to will be the breaking and the making of us. He will break our independence and self-reliance. He will break the power of our own soul. He will make us both a warrior, and a son (generic) of His love. Process is our own personal action plan for growth and development.

We learn in process that the purpose of problems is to produce faith. The aim in allowing demonic opposition is to develop power and authority in us. The intention behind human opposition is that God will use it to teach us grace. Tribulation is designed to produce patience and endurance. The objective behind conflict is to increase God's love in our hearts and bring us to full maturity in His nature. When God allows temptation (that doesn't mean He causes it — He cannot tempt) He seeks for us to be advanced in righteousness. When our resources come under attack, He teaches us how to give so that all our needs can be supplied in Christ. Process is where we discover God to be all that He ever said and all we will ever need.

Assignment

❋ Make a list of the current areas of struggle and difficulty; what is being revealed to you in Christ?

❋ What prophetic words have been spoken over you? What are the key descriptive words and phrases that point to your identity?

❋ What is the Holy Spirit processing in your life at this time which is in line with this identity being formed in you?

Commission

❋ What attribute does God want to cultivate in you? What is the problem he will use to develop it? What is His intention? How must you cooperate?

❈ Develop an action plan for all your processing so that you become focused and obedient in your lifestyle. Example:

Attribute	Problem	Intention	Cooperation
Faith	Financial resources are under attack.	To teach us how to give.	Learn to sow and reap.
Grace	A difficult relationship with a person who is against me.	To enable me to love like Jesus. Not give like for like.	Learn how to move in the opposite spirit. Be gracious, kind and loving.
Sovereignty of God	Spiritual opposition, prolonged attack.	To discover majesty of God and stand in His steadfast spirit.	Learn endurance and praise under pressure.

Personal Notes

❄ Action Plan.

Attribute	Problem Area	God's Intention	My Cooperation

Knowledge without Experience is Not Truth

A warrior is a seeker after Truth. We want freedom above all else. We seek to release captives. To open blind eyes and create an awareness of God in all His beauty and excellence. Warriors want territory. They seek a land of their own. They want the city, the region, the state/province, the country, and the nations. They want war. They seek battle. They have a passionate love for Jesus and an equal hatred of the enemy. We come to destroy the devil and all his works.

Jesus came to reveal the Father. His goal was to open up and establish the Kingdom of Heaven on earth. He came to model a righteous life — as a man before God — pre-Cross. His intention was to create a supernatural lifestyle that was physical and practical. He wanted to disciple and mentor a generation of leaders and warriors. He came to battle against a religious system that took everything from people but did not give them a direct encounter with God. He came, of course, to die for us — to be the sacrificial lamb of God that would save us from our sins. He came to rise from the dead and be our intercessor and provider before the throne of His Father.

He came, of course, to be the fullness of our truth and experience. "I am the way, the truth, and the life!" [John 14:6] "He who has seen me, has seen the Father." [John 14:9] "As He is, so are we in this world." [1 John 4:17] To be Christlike is to be the same as Jesus in all things. We cannot separate Him from the supernatural lifestyle that He still models. In the same way that we are in Him, we too, cannot be separated from healings, miracles, signs, and wonders.

> *"Truly, truly, I say to you, he who believes in Me, the works that I do, he will do also; and greater works than these he will do; because I go to the Father.*
>
> *"Whatever you ask in My name, that will I do, so that the Father may be glorified in the Son.*
>
> *"If you ask Me anything in My name, I will do it. [John 14:12-14]*

Like Jesus, we depend upon the Father for all things. We can do nothing outside of our position in Christ. Christ is our life [Colossians 1:4a], and we model in ourselves His relationship with the Father [John 5:19-20]. The Holy Spirit is our Helper in all things Christlike [John 14:26; 15:26-27].

When Jesus revealed His Life Message [from Isaiah 61] He did not do so as part of His Sermon on the Mount. Instead He went to His hometown church to talk about His relationship with the Holy Spirit:

> *And Jesus returned to Galilee in the power of the Spirit, and news about Him spread through all the surrounding district.*
>
> *And He began teaching in their synagogues and was praised by all.*
>
> *And He came to Nazareth, where He had been brought up; and as was His custom, He entered*

the synagogue on the Sabbath, and stood up to read.

And the book of the prophet Isaiah was handed to Him. And He opened the book and found the place where it was written,

"THE SPIRIT OF THE LORD IS UPON ME,
BECAUSE HE ANOINTED ME TO PREACH THE GOSPEL TO THE POOR.
HE HAS SENT ME TO PROCLAIM RELEASE TO THE CAPTIVES,
AND RECOVERY OF SIGHT TO THE BLIND,
TO SET FREE THOSE WHO ARE OPPRESSED,
TO PROCLAIM THE FAVORABLE YEAR OF THE LORD."

And He closed the book, gave it back to the attendant and sat down; and the eyes of all in the synagogue were fixed on Him.

And He began to say to them, "Today this Scripture has been fulfilled in your hearing."
[Luke 4:14-21]

Part of His ministry was to take a stand against religiosity in church leadership. "Woe" is a primary exclamation of grief and also of denunciation. In Matthew 23:13-29, He used it on eight occasions. He called church leaders hypocrites, blind men, blind guides, and whited sepulchres. His foremost accusation [verse 23] was that they shut off the kingdom of heaven from people because they had no experience of it themselves.

In mentoring the disciples, He was developing a church leadership that could carry the message and lifestyle of the kingdom in themselves.

He taught them how to believe God, how to move in the supernatural, how to have power over the enemy, and how to love the people and release them into a lifestyle of blessing and favor.

He did not teach them how to do meetings. He taught them how to be good examples of a kingdom lifestyle.

He stood against a religious system that had captured people in a legalistic environment that prevented them from being loved fully by God. When the system defines the experience we can have with God, then we have no freedom. Jesus came to set us free from an organized religious experience that teaches us how to think, speak, and act before God. It is the role of the Holy Spirit to renew our minds, not for man to program them. Jesus came to overthrow a system that does not allow us the joy of exposure to His fullness, anointing, and glory. We have an entry into the eternal kingdom of the Lord Jesus Christ, abundantly supplied by Him.

> *Grace and peace be multiplied to you in the knowledge of God and of Jesus our Lord; seeing that His divine power has granted to us everything pertaining to life and godliness, through the true knowledge of Him who called us by His own glory and excellence.*

For by these He has granted to us His precious and magnificent promises, so that by them you may become partakers of the divine nature, having escaped the corruption that is in the world by lust.

Now for this very reason also, applying all diligence, in your faith supply moral excellence, and in your moral excellence, knowledge, and in your knowledge, self-control, and in your self-control, perseverance, and in your perseverance, godliness,

and in your godliness, brotherly kindness, and in your brotherly kindness, love.

For if these qualities are yours and are increasing, they render you neither useless nor unfruitful in the true knowledge of our Lord Jesus Christ.

For he who lacks these qualities is blind or short-sighted, having forgotten his purification from his former sins.

Therefore, brethren, be all the more diligent to make certain about His calling and choosing you; for as long as you practice these things, you will never stumble;

for in this way the entrance into the eternal kingdom of our Lord and Savior Jesus Christ will be abundantly supplied to you.

[2 Peter 1:2-11]

An abundant life involves multiplication. It is concerned with living an accelerated lifestyle within the permissions of God. In Christ, everything is "yes and amen" from the Father's heart. He has granted us so much in His Son. We have permission and also formal rights on the Kingdom by virtue of being included in Christ. The Father is in complete agreement regarding our position, status, and inheritance in and through the Lord Jesus Christ. He loves to honor Jesus in this way. "To grant" literally means to "consent to support". God is saying yes to us. Warriors live in the permissions of God.

Everything that our life and calling requires for us to follow and serve God wholeheartedly, will be supplied in Jesus' Name. We are developing a habit of faith based upon a true knowledge of God. There are levels of knowledge, obviously. All knowledge gained must be accompanied by an experience. Only the truth can set us free. Knowledge without experience is merely true. Knowing it in our head does not change our mindset. Knowing it in our heart [inner man] and experiencing the power and release of it in our circumstances, makes it truth.

Head knowledge is one level. Academic understanding is another. Never trust a theologian who has not experienced truth for himself. Logical, rational, and intellectual appreciation of scripture will not take us into the high places of faith and breakthrough. A true knowledge of God is based on a relationship that has proved the intentions of the Father in the physical, natural level of life situations.

I have been healed physically many times by the Lord. I have moved in supernatural revelatory gifts for more than three decades. I have received financial provisions totaling millions of dollars. I have had the fun of donating millions of dollars to kingdom projects. I have proven experience in living a life of faith. A true knowledge of God must lead us into a direct, physical encounter with the Lord.

The most important purpose of the Father is that we experience His glory and excellence as a part of our own calling [verse 3]. We do not represent an inferior kingdom. We are not helpless and hopeless. The God who gives knowledge that creates medical breakthroughs, loves to surprise us with outbreaks of power from another dimension … the spirit.

Healings, miracles, signs, and wonders are all physical breakthroughs that cannot be rationalized. Sometimes the Father has no intention of explaining Himself. Faith is beyond reason and far superior to intellect. It is a glorious thing to see people healed physically — to witness the resurrection of physical capability in Jesus' Name. Glory and excellence is the only way to represent the majesty, sovereignty, and supremacy of heaven.

Our problem as evangelicals is that we believe that the kingdom is only spiritual. We do not believe that it is also physical, mental, and emotional. It is for the whole man. We compound our unbelief by trying to access this kingdom from a cerebral viewpoint. So we water down the spirituality of the kingdom by using our reason as a prime means of interpreting God's heart.

Then we elevate scripture above the Lord Jesus Christ by referring to the bible as the word of God ... when scripture actually says the opposite [John 1:1-5; 1 John 1:1-4; John 1:14-18; Revelation 19:11-13]. Then we replace the Holy Spirit with the bible because, obviously, now we have a book; we don't need God! Then, because we have no spiritual dimension of interpreting scripture, we fall back on logic, and rationale rather than wisdom. We have a knowledge of God but no power to relate to Him in a way that changes our environment. We are reduced to explaining Him rather than experiencing Him. How far have we fallen from the Early Church! Where is the glory and excellence of God in His body?

Scripture is within truth. The Words of God in written form. The Word of God is a person [Revelation 19:11-13; John 1:1 and 14]. Jesus said of Himself, "I am the Way, the Truth, and the Life." [John 14:6] The Word and the Truth are one person, Jesus Christ.

Freedom occurs when we receive Truth and develop a relationship with it that leads to transformation. For that to happen we must receive Truth in the shape, identity and personality of Jesus. He becomes that Truth to me, in me and for me.

I cannot take the truth and apply it to myself. This is self help. Which self is applying the truth? Instead, Jesus lives that truth in me. I surrender to His life and He becomes the Living Word in my spirit and soul. I am wonderfully impacted by His presence spiritually, emotionally, physically and mentally. My whole person is affected by His Whole Person. Too many Christians only give mental assent to truth. Cerebral acceptance is not an experience. The joy of the Lord is a relational encounter with His exuberant happiness. We live under His smile and our hearts are light.

He is the Truth and fully makes His abode in me using that truth. [John 14:23] The Holy Spirit leads me into all Truth [John 16:23] by empowering me to have a relationship with Jesus in the particular area that He is changing in me.

The way we come into salvation is the way that this salvation is sustained. Jesus as the Living Word is presented to us as Savior. When we receive Jesus personally as Savior, we become saved. Salvation is a person living within us. Anyone who has not received Him as a personal savior, even if they know all the scriptures, is not saved. What is true in one area of spirituality, is true in all. The Word and the Truth are a person that must be invited into our lives and fully received. The question is not, "Do you know about Jesus," but "Have you received Him?" For the Truth to set us free, we must continue to receive it as a person.

For example, if we want to experience the real peace of God, then memorizing scriptures about peace or studying the subject will not achieve that objective. We study to show ourselves approved when we want to teach others and guide them into an experience of God [2 Timothy 2:15].

Memorizing scriptures about peace will not lead me into an experience of peace. When Jesus by His presence becomes my Prince of Peace then I am set free to be peaceful. Truth has an identity attached to it. We experience God relationally in all matters of truth and spirituality. This is what it means to be Christlike. He has made His abode in me. He lives in my experience because I encounter His personality in the Truth He established in me. He is my experience. We call it Godliness.

Godliness is about experiencing the wonderful nature of God in all of life. It is knowing with certainty that God has made provision for all eventualities that we will face. A warrior does not let go of splendor. They refuse to be downgraded from the truth.

We have been granted precious and magnificent promises so that by them we can partake of the nature of Jesus [verse 4]. The promises of God, when they become a reality, lead us into godliness — a revelatory experience so profound it changes our whole character and personality. We become transformed. We experience a marked change in nature, form, and appearance.

Transformation is the process by which a person is converted into another of greater value. In biology, transformation is the genetic alteration of a cell, by introduction of extraneous DNA. Spiritually, transformation occurs by the renewing of our mind [Romans 12:2]. That means at some point, we must cease to use logic as the prime means of understanding God and His Kingdom. Logic, as the prime means of understanding, has been superseded by the wisdom from above. We are to be renewed in the spirit of our mind [Ephesians 4:23].

How the Lord thinks is the model for our own thought life. We have the mind of Christ. Jesus thought, spoke, and acted in faith, which is the language and behavior of Heaven. He saw what His Father did, and His own actions were compatible. He spoke the way He heard it from the Father. Knowledge must become experience, or we are not changed. Only the truth can set us free. The key to knowledge is experience. This actually was the charge that Jesus made in His denouncement of religiosity to the Pharisees:

> *Woe to you lawyers! For you have taken away the key of knowledge; you yourselves did not enter, and you hindered those who were entering." [Luke 11:52]*

God deliver us from people who teach truth but have no experience of it. Their lack of experience in the truth prevents people from seeing the opportunity that the Father is presenting. One of the saddest talks I ever heard was a man teaching about the Holy Spirit, who clearly did not have a relationship with Him. It was pitiful; and totally, mind-numbingly boring!

When we practice the Presence of God, we can never stumble. Godliness is the Presence of God personified in our hearts and minds. We do not become a new person by changing our behavior; we discover the person we already are in Christ and behave accordingly. That was the wisdom taught me by one of my mentors in 1978. Truth walks with you and replenishes your experience of God at different levels of life.

How many sermons have we listened to over the years? How many have caused us to see God as He really is? How many have set us free to be loved by God differently? How many have been backed up by supernatural ministry that has resulted in a breakthrough over our lives? What have we learned and experienced of the majesty, sovereignty, and supremacy of God in our lives? Do we know our place in the kingdom? Do we understand anything of the intentionality of the Father towards us in Christ?

Are we astonished, amazed, and full of wonder about the Father? Are we living above our circumstances? Has faith increased? Are we confident about God's passion for us?

Assignment

❋ Be honest about your current experience of God. Do you know more about how the church operates than how God works?

❋ What is your current experience of the Kingdom of Heaven?

❋ What was the last truth you were taught, that actually set you free in your circumstances?

Commission

❋ Are you being equipped to do the work of ministry?

❋ Are you being mentored in your devotion, relationship, and worship of God?

❋ What do you need God to do for you that empowers you to live the life you have always wanted in Christ?

❋ Ask the Father to send you a Helper who can lead you into all truth [John 14:16-17].

Personal Notes

The Mystery of Godliness

Grace is the opening up of a new place so that we can live responsively in alignment with the Father, through Jesus Christ, by the Holy Spirit. Spiritual warriors perfect the art of bouncing back. They know that a crisis leads to elevation. What is trying to take us down will, in fact, cause us to rise up — in God!

A crisis attracts the power and strength of God. *And He has said to me, "My grace is sufficient for you, for power is perfected in weakness." Most gladly, therefore, I will rather boast about my weaknesses, so that the power of Christ may dwell in me.*

Therefore I am well content with weaknesses, with insults, with distresses, with persecutions, with difficulties, for Christ's sake; for when I am weak, then I am strong. [2 Corinthians 12:9]

Our cooperation with that is to enable the Holy Spirit to empower us, so that our attitude comes into agreement with God's intention. Because they love the learning, warriors are released through joy to enter the right paradigm for personal growth.

We can gladly boast about who God is for us in the face of our own inadequacies. We can be satisfied and at ease with God's process because of our delight in the Holy Spirit. What we are being shown about Jesus, and our place in Him, is so thrilling to us; it takes us into a new dimension of response.

Jesus is everything to us. He is our place and our position before the Father. We are in Him. He is for us. The very core of our existence is made available through Christ. Everything comes to us from the Father by Jesus. We exist for the Father through Jesus.

> *"Yet for us there is but one God, the Father, from whom are all things and we exist for Him; and one Lord, Jesus Christ, by whom are all things, and we exist through Him."*
> *[1 Corinthians 8:6]*

We abide in Christ for the sake of the Father. He gets to completely fulfill His heart for us, as He does for the Lord Jesus. I am loved in the same way that Jesus is loved. We cannot receive anything in and of ourselves. Everything is joyfully given to us by the Father through Jesus [John 3:27].

Everything originates in God [1 Corinthians 11:12], and it is the Father's good pleasure to give us the kingdom [Luke 12:32]. This is such an important truth, especially for performance — driven believers, who feel they need to earn their salvation (which actually is not of works, lest anyone become boastful) [Ephesians 2:9].

> *Or WHO HAS FIRST GIVEN TO HIM THAT IT MIGHT BE PAID BACK TO HIM AGAIN?*
> *For from Him and through Him and to Him are all things. To Him be the glory forever. Amen.*
> *[Romans 11:35-36]*

It is describing a cycle. Everything comes from God, through Christ in us and goes back to God. We give to God the very thing He wants from us, which He gives us in the first place. This also is in our DNA. How many of us who are parents, when it is our birthday, have given our children money to buy us a gift?

This is exactly what the Father is like. He freely gives us, what He most wants from us. "We love Him **because** He first loved us."

[1 John 4:19]

Every good thing given and every perfect gift is from above, coming down from the Father of lights, with whom there is no variation or shifting shadow. [James 1:17]

The Father is consistent about everything. He is and does. He will never act outside of His nature or character. There is no change in Him. "I am the Lord, I change not." He remains the same as He has always been [Hebrews 13:8]. Every gift of God exemplifies His goodness to us. The Holy Spirit loves to emphasize the beauty of the Godhead. It is our role in the earth to be astonished among men. The Good News is so astounding, so amazing; it often feels like we're captured in a fairy tale. It sounds and seems too good to be true. The truth is so overwhelming, so bright, so glorious, we have to wear sunglasses in worship. The bible is such a fabulous book; it reads like a fantasy novel — only one that is so enchanting, so fascinatingly thrilling, we have to keep smelling salts next to it, to revive us when we're overcome by goodness. We read scripture to discover what God is really, really like and when we do, we get filled up by His beauty and radiance. Worship is not a choice; it's an explosion that pours out of us. It's impossible not to worship, when the revelation we are receiving is so glorious, we cannot contain our response. We would have to strain and stress every muscle to be able to contain rejoicing. Try holding your breath for as long as you possibly can — it is utterly impossible ... we explode from within. Real worship is like that; our inner man seeks a release, an expression towards God.

Every thought is drawn to Him. We are pulled into His glory. His lovingkindness is so magnetic it pulls us towards Him, like iron filings to a magnet. Every fiber of our being is both challenged and captivated by His love. The glory of God is that He is so irresistibly beautiful, we are captured by the goodness that radiates out of Him. He pulls love from all our hidden places of the heart, soul, mind, and body [Luke 10:27]. The best form of evangelism is to be a lover of God. Everyone loves a love story. To love others the way God loves you is the height of the gospel. It's undeniable Good News.

When we are fully and completely loved, we relax. It is so vital for us to win the internal battle of acceptance over performance. However we plan to serve God, we do so because we are radically loved, not to try to earn His love. Love makes givers of us all. We must settle into the love of God; be warmed and filled by it; allow it to seep into every pore or our personality. Every cut, every gash of our woundedness, of mind and heart, needs to be refreshed by love. In this way we cease to be present/past in our focus for life. Our past is not a rerun of our history. We are set free, delivered by love.

We can become present/future in our relationship with the Father. Fully loved and accepted in the present with a great future to look forward to. As He is, so are we in this world.

[1 John 4:17]

The reality and the experience of that love is so powerful it radically alters our complexion. Our character and personality are adjusted by love so completely, that we literally become a new person.

A whole, new powerful state of being emerges in our hearts and lives. We become content. That is, we enter a state of peaceful happiness by which we view all things. Two of the most powerful change elements in the universe are godliness and contentment.

> *But godliness actually is a means of great gain when accompanied by contentment.*
>
> *[1 Timothy 6:6]*

An individual has arrived in the spirit when both of these are present and growing. Godliness in the Old Testament is used to describe a person who had a lifestyle that was a practical exhibition of lovingkindness towards people who are misfortunate, and whom it is in our power to help. Even at our own expense of time, money, convenience, religion, and national prejudice.

It depicts a person who consciously and deliberately reveals the lovingkindness, steadfast love, grace, mercy, faithfulness, and goodness of the Lord. God's kindness provides the power and strength by which our lives are to be directed. This is Godliness, and the Father has a special attachment to people who live this way.

> But know that the LORD has set apart the godly
> man for Himself;
> The LORD hears when I call to Him.
> [Psalm 4:3]

This means that God deals wonderfully with people who deal wonderfully! Being like God opens us up to Him on an even more dynamic level. Thus, God is able to be more dynamic towards us which results in us being more radical in how we love others. Exponential growth is a factor of the kingdom and a king who adores abundance! When we have a revelation of the majesty of the Lord's goodness, the experience of that impacts our lives in a deeply practical way. An experience of revelation must result in God's words becoming works in us. The Father shows His faith in Jesus by His works in us. He would never require it of us, that we demonstrate faith by works [James 2:18] if He Himself did not live by the same value [1Thessolians 2:13].

In the New Testament, Godliness marks the relationship in which we stand before God and He stands towards us. We are in Christ, and our position in

Him is secure. "Of God are you in Christ." [1 Corinthians 1:30] By the Father's doing we celebrate life in the Son. The Father is the foundation of our promise and the provision for our life. He has decreed that He will supply all our needs according to His riches in glory by Christ Jesus [Philippians 4:19].

Spiritual warriors know their position in Christ and how to maintain their place of favor and anointing. They exercise themselves for the purpose of godliness. They practice their revelation through their experience of it, giving themselves to cultivating the right spirit at all times [1 timothy 4:7]. Godliness refers to a person who has a reverence for the goodness of God. They believe in the Father's goodness implicitly; they depend on it. Anyone living in godliness as a lifestyle is going to prosper. Godliness holds all the promises of God both for the present life (today) and the life to come (tomorrow)! [1 Timothy 4:8]

Godliness is connected to our becoming like Jesus. We become heart-focused and directed. Warriors have a sacred awe and a reverent lifestyle that demonstrates the nature of God. They have a Godward attitude that is focused on pleasing the Father. This is what Jesus is like. He only said and did what the Father was speaking and doing. He was a normal, righteous man who behaved perfectly before God. He was not God pretending to be a man; He was a man! He had a fabulous perspective on the Father. He had a dynamic relationship with God that enabled Him to be trusted and empowered. He had a Godward attitude that was focused on pleasing the Father.

Godliness is something of a mystery to many people [1 Timothy 3:16]. It is the revelation of the nature of God that provokes a powerful lifestyle and a spiritual focus from another dimension of reality — the kingdom pressing into us, a spirit of wisdom and revelation in the knowledge of Him, that calls forth an enlightenment so provocative that we are lifted into a different spiritual state [Ephesians 1:17-21].

Godliness is our opportunity to live a heaven-sent life on earth, to live a life above, to be governed by the inner man and the disclosures of heaven. This is the doctrine of godliness that Paul is mentoring in Timothy [1 Timothy 6:3]. Doctrines are a set of values that govern our lifestyle and personality. We are wonderfully ruled from within and powerfully expressive of this life from without.

Godliness is a revelatory, experiential power that touches people bringing healing, restoration, and release. Virtue flowed out of Jesus when He was touched by a sick woman [Luke 8:43-46]. Godliness is the tangible presence of God. People can observe it, be touched and overwhelmed by it. A doctrine teaches by example, and by a lifestyle observed. Paul often said, "...the things you have heard and seen in me ... do". This is doctrine — exampled teaching [Philippians 4:9], not taught in a classroom but in life circumstances.

For this reason I also suffer these things, but I am not ashamed; for I know whom I have believed and I am convinced that He is able to guard what I have entrusted to Him until that day.

Retain the standard of sound words which you have heard from me, in the faith and love which are in Christ Jesus.

Guard, through the Holy Spirit who dwells in us, the treasure which has been entrusted to you.

Trust is a two way street. We get to trust God with things that are of real value to us. He trusts us with His own treasure which we guard with help from our Heavenly friend. Only God could be as wonderful as this. He allows us to live within His own example. He is our model, example, and therefore our guarantee. We live a life of conviction regarding His nature, character, and integrity.

It is for freedom that Christ has set us free. Our freedom means everything to the Holy Spirit. His role is to take the things of Jesus and show them to us [John 15:26; John 16:7-15]. Godliness is the product, the evidence of the Holy Spirit at work in us.

Warriors love the Holy Spirit as much as Jesus does. They lean into Him for Comfort and Truth. Their love is revelatory intuition that takes their perception of the Father to a higher level of experience. In all things the Father has provided us with a life that transcends all our difficulties. He comes to us; to be something for us that lifts us up to the place where He abides.

Assignment

* Describe the nature that most attracts you to Him; that makes you feel most relaxed and accepted in Him.
* In your areas of current struggle, how is the Father viewing you personally?
* What plans does the Father have for your freedom and success in these areas?
* How will you cooperate with the Holy Spirit in godliness?

Commission

* Godliness is being the same to others as God is to you.
* Using Romans 11:35-36 as your guide, what are you currently receiving from the Lord?
* How is Jesus developing that in you?
* How will you release that back to the Lord so that He receives glory?

Personal Notes

Contentment: The Outward Expression
of an Inward Glory

The most powerful mentors in my life all had one thing in common, and it has released a hunger in my own heart. They gazed at the Lord with a childlike simplicity and wonder. They had an innocence about them — a simple purity, humility, grace, and a deep abiding love for Jesus that was naked to the eye, a visible passion that ruled each day.

I cried out for that — fasted and prayed, hungered for it to the point of obsession. Children who are loved powerfully, never worry. They have a glorious complacency. An assurance so profound, it rests. An inability to be anxious — Father is here.

Choosing not to worry is actually an act of worship. We cast all our burdens onto Him because we trust His great heart toward us. Our trust leads us to do good to others because the fun part of faith is loaning it to people who have none. To abide is to simply be content to remain in Christ where the Father has placed us. This is one of the most powerful disciplines that we possess in the Holy Spirit.

To dwell in the land of promise, the place of God's goodness and lovingkindness — this is part of our favor. That which God has placed us in, is the place of our remaining. We cherish His provision in Jesus, and we cultivate His faithfulness. The Holy Spirit is intentional about delight. The entire Godhead lives with a calm, joyous, untroubled sense of delight in themselves and all that they have created.

When we live in delight before the Lord, it releases our inheritance. Delight begets desire [Psalm 37:4]. Desire is a consequence of enjoyment, the fruit of gladness in God. Warriors know how trust affects the heart of God. He is thrilled at faith. What Father is not enchanted by the dependence of a small child?

I loved watching my children grow up. Ben had a wide-eyed innocence. He would sit for hours, contented on my lap, as I read him book after book. He knew every book by heart. I would sometimes leave out a section, and he would clap his hands in delight and correct me in his piping little voice.

Seth would crawl into my lap, up my chest and lay on me, his head on my shoulder, making snuffling noises into my neck. He would stay there all the time except when he wanted to play super heroes. I expect you can guess who the villain was.

Sophie had these incredible eyes and a smile that would melt an iceberg. She shared everything. Every sorrow, every happy thing she shared equally. She would come, stand before me, lift her arms, and look at me — irresistible.

Years later, in the Spirit, learning to live before God as a much-loved child, all these memories came back to train me. I caught the sense of enchantment in the Father. His deep affection moved me to tears. His joy in me changed my life. His kindness is so overwhelming on days that I'm left dabbing my eyes with a handkerchief.

The joy in simply trusting is such a fabulous experience. I wonder that people don't do it more. Why do some people have to be persuaded to trust the Lord? To have a conversation with Him about my life and current events in the ministry is such a huge privilege. To hear His wisdom in return and then to sit and meditate on the whole experience — amazing.

I adore wisdom. I'm hooked on God's perception of my life. It has seeped into the cracks in my heart and the pores of my skin. The Father's way of seeing and thinking is so magnetic, it draws me. It is exhilarating, life-changing. It slows down my heart rate, makes me relaxed, peaceful. It leads me into trust, opens up my faith place, makes me rejoice. It is so easy to understand why Jesus only said what the Father was saying. His words are so beautiful, powerful, exceptional. There are certain God thoughts that I totally love sharing — perceptions that empower the listener, words that actually produce life in people. Occasionally the Lord lets me hear the sound His words make on a hungry heart or a thirsty soul. I have been out in the dry, arid wilderness when it rained. Stood naked in a downpour, listening to the land say, "Thank you, thank you." Watched green shoots come through the soil almost immediately, seen the land transformed in a day. It's the same sound — absolute life, begetting life.

To be encouraged to commit life to the Father and then further empowered to give thanks as a mark of trust is a brilliant daily occurrence in devotion. God is good and His love empowers forever.

The Holy Spirit gathers all our emotions, thoughts, and affections about the Father and puts them into one place. It's called contentment. Godliness and contentment together are priceless. The power is exponential. You move out of the country where God adds to you, and you take up residence in the land of multiplication.

I have learned over many years how to live by faith, How to pray in food, money, and resources. The budgets that the Father set for life and ministry were always greater than my income. I had to learn the peace of a nil balance in finances. Every month, He would make sure that I could never take an ounce of comfort from my bank statement. Comfort is His alone to give, and He guards it jealously. I learned to obey His voice, to give when He requested, to give in the face of my own need, and to be at peace about it. I learned the Godliness in believing, obeying, and trusting. I came to adore the nature of God in giving.

Ironically, the issue I most struggled with was prosperity. I had problems with abundance. The Father patiently got me past my religious explanations and made me see that there was a part of me that thought I was unworthy. The parts about ourselves that we least like have the most love reserved for them from the

Father. He took me away from false humility and taught me to enjoy money and possessions. I don't love money; I love what money can do in the hands of a loving God. I love God and money together: doing good, helping out, blessing people.

Jesus, by blessing and encouraging a hateful man who had defrauded his whole community, brought that village into financial prosperity. When He touched the life of Zaccheus [Luke 19] money flowed into homes and families. Half his goods he gave to the poor. Where he had defrauded people, he repaid them 400%. He got his heart back; and the people around him, robbed of their prosperity, were restored to dignity.

The Father changes our perceptions, and our mindset shifts into a different gear. When our mind is renewed, our life is transformed; and our heart is forever adjusted upwards. I came into a place of utter contentment, and I ceased to worry. Contentment is a state of peaceful happiness.

It is the satisfaction of having our expectations realized. We have learned to trust the Lord. He is faithful, and we know it by experience. Contentment occurs when we realize the fullness of God's heart towards us. We take pleasure in His deep affection. We are His Beloved.

The Father fully discharges His obligation to Christ: in us, to us, and by the Holy Spirit through us. They do so with great enjoyment. It's a conspiracy of kindness, and we are the object of their passion. They make true their intentions. They teach us to trust their nature; that is how we become Godly. When we add their nature to our satisfaction, life blossoms; and we are content in the hands of a loving God. The Father abounds towards us; and we may abound towards others, to draw them too, into the place of trusting.

> *And God is able to make all grace abound to you, so that always having all sufficiency in everything, you may have an abundance for every good deed.*
> *[2 Corinthians 9:8]*

Out of our own sufficiency we can begin to bless, support, and prosper others. Their journey into trust and faith begins with a gift that opens them up to the claims of God. A gift makes way for the giver [Proverbs 18:16]; this is true on lots of levels.

It is vital that people come into abundance because then the blessing on the poor can become exponential. Our increase will advance somebody else. If we do not allow ourselves to expand in the goodness of God, the poor cannot be enlarged effectively. We can bless them periodically, but we cannot take them out of poverty. That demands a different approach to giving.

There is a lifestyle in the Kingdom that can affect our community. People need to see the riches of God, not just economically, but also in health terms, emotional release, hope, love, joy, and peace. The willingness of God to empower people is enormous.

Contentment is a big part of our revelation of the nature of God.

Contentment works in reverse too. It is not just a revelation that works when things are going well. It works in all places and all circumstances.

> *Not that I speak from want, for I have learned*
> *to be content in whatever circumstances I am.*
> *I know how to get along with humble means,*
> *and I also know how to live in prosperity; in*
> *any and every circumstance I have learned the*
> *secret of being filled and going hungry, both of*
> *having abundance and suffering need.*
> *I can do all things through Him who*
> *strengthens me. [Philippians 4:11-13]*

There have been many times on my travels, especially into communist countries where supplies were low, or developing nations where they were non-existent, where I encountered overwhelming poverty. In some places we were able to bring supplies with us or buy goods in the country ourselves. Always, always we blessed people's food/store cupboards in prayer. We claimed land, removed curses, blessed the seed, and the water supply. I have chopped down trees, thrown them into polluted rivers, and prayed for the water. Then, of course you have to be the first to drink it. For a few days you are a human Petri dish, and everyone observes your stupidity or faith, fellow missionaries and all! If you're not dead or vomiting by the third day, everyone happily drinks also.

I have located underground water supplies by words of knowledge and dug out wells, moving communities in Africa to new land that could provide food and sweet grazing for cattle.

In these situations our own contentment with God is a powerful weapon against the enemy. Contentment must be passed on. When I see people in poverty I am not content to leave them there. My own contentment militates against a spirit of poverty, and I have to contend against it. Supplying food is one answer. Teaching farming and animal husbandry is another. Buying land and building orphan communities around farming and businesses is a better model. People need a self-sustaining lifestyle, not a succession of handouts. I believe in emergency feeding, but self respect and dignity comes with enlargement.

When I am in the midst of a poor community, I do not feel guilty for my own prosperity. God does not do guilt. I allow my own contentment to be released in a warfare capacity. The kingdom is concerned with the business of warfare. A kingdom mindset is the same as a business mindset. How do we create wealth so that we can kill poverty? We do not give to people so they can remain poor. We must ensure that our generosity does not empower people to remain in crisis. We teach them to abound so that they can enfranchise another individual/family/community out of poverty into contentment.

Of course in these circumstances, while we are planning and strategizing, I am content to eat the same food or go hungry, if there is none. I have encountered involuntary fasting on many occasions, and I have eaten some enterprising food stuffs! Saying grace takes on a whole new meaning in such situations. It is the first line of defense in spiritual warfare. The old missionary prayer of, "Lord, I'll get it down. You keep it down," still holds true!

Contentment maintains delight. Curry powder covers a multitude of interesting dishes. Always take some spices, then you don't have to think about what you're eating. God makes us glad. Gladness of heart is a powerful weapon against the enemy who has no access to joy — it's a fruit of the spirit. His only happiness lies in misery, poverty, human degradation, and enslavement. A glad heart gives joy and respect to people.

Some of my best memories of interaction in foreign cultures have been squatting around open fires, cooking, laughing, eating with people whose language I did not understand. Love and joy have a language of their own. Contentment in those circumstances endeared me to people and opened up their hearts.

We live in a world geared towards discontent. Most advertising is built upon creating a need based around dissatisfaction. An unreal world is created, of which we are not a part, unless we purchase the product that makes us acceptable. Retail therapy is supposed to make us happy. Our self-worth depends upon being seen in the right places with the right people. In order for someone to be "in", someone else, by definition, has to be "out". Hardly Christian, and not worth the effort.

Contentment is so much more than possession and recognition. How we perceive ourselves is an assessment best derived from a revelation of God. When we know who the Father is in Himself, we get a true idea of value. The Holy Spirit teaches us to see ourselves in the person of Jesus. As He is, so are we. Made in His image. We give life to one another by our perception. We create a value that can embrace people in the love of God.

Contentment, the capacity to live in a state of peaceful happiness with the Lord, yourself, and others.

Assignment

* What are your current areas of personal discontent?
* Where are the areas in relationship where you have not been accepted?
* What would you most like to change about yourself?

Commission

❋ What would contentment look like for you …
describe.

❋ What is the Father's perception of you …
summarize.

❋ Write a psalm of thanksgiving to the Lord in
joyful recognition of all His good thoughts about
you.

Personal Notes

Everything Leads to Majesty

We are in the process, aided by the Holy Spirit, of discovering a revelation of God so profound, it governs every facet of our lives. In line with these perceptions, we cultivate experiences of God's nature that empower us to breakthrough obstacles, overcome the enemy, and overwhelm human opposition with the goodness of God.

When we see the sovereignty of God, we are empowered to love our enemies. When we are captivated by majesty, we develop more faith. Our certainties concerning God's nature are the bedrock of empowerment in ministry.

Paul embraced his crisis situations: "If we suffer, we shall also reign with Him" [2 Timothy 2:2].

> *The Spirit Himself testifies with our spirit that we are children of God,*
> *and if children, heirs also, heirs of God and fellow heirs with Christ, if indeed we suffer with Him so that we may also be glorified with Him.*
> *For I consider that the sufferings of this present time are not worthy to be compared with the glory that is to be revealed to us.*
> *For the anxious longing of the creation waits eagerly for the revealing of the sons of God.*
> *[Romans 8:16-19]*

This is not a revelatory experience for a future time but a present exposure to the intentionality of God. We are living in eternity now. I have been experiencing eternal life in Christ since the day of salvation. On earth, as it is in Heaven. As He is, so are we. Greater miracles than His will we do. Eternity now! We are present day partakers of the divine nature.

The anxious longing of the creation waits eagerly for the revealing of the sons of God. The sun longs for another command (as Joshua) for it to stand still in the heavens while he had enough light for warfare — that's majesty! [Joshua 10:12-14].

Wind and waves love to obey the commands of God [Mark 4:39-41]. Creation loves to be part of God doing the impossible [2 Kings 6:4-7].

Peter knew that where majesty is present, glory is not far behind. They are inseparable. On the other side of crisis, glory is everpresent.

> *Beloved, do not be surprised at the fiery ordeal among you, which comes upon you for your testing, as though some strange thing were happening to you;*
>
> *but to the degree that you share the sufferings of Christ, keep on rejoicing, so that also at the revelation of His glory you may rejoice with exultation.*
>
> *If you are reviled for the name of Christ, you are blessed, because the Spirit of glory and of God rests on you. [1 Peter 4:12-14]*

Obviously, all tests teach us something about the Lord and ourselves. Every test gives us a window into the majesty and supremacy of the Lord. The majesty of God is more sharply defined in a crunch situation. Indeed, what if all critical circumstances contain the possibility of rapid advancement through majesty? In the renewing of our mind, we are constantly coming face-to-face with the matchless Presence of God.

Majesty must dominate mindsets. In crisis, the spirit of glory rests upon us — a radiant idea of God so magnificent it rules the enemy from our inner man of the spirit. Cascading joy erupts in our hearts at the mere thought of the Father's unrivalled invincibility.

The eyes of our inner man are opened to discover the surpassing greatness of God's power to us who are ready to believe.

> *I pray that the eyes of your heart may be enlightened, so that you will know what is the hope of His calling, what are the riches of the glory of His inheritance in the saints,*
> *and what is the surpassing greatness of His power toward us who believe. These are in accordance with the working of the strength of His might*
> *which He brought about in Christ, when He raised Him from the dead and seated Him at His right hand in the heavenly places,*

far above all rule and authority and power and
dominion, and every name that is named, not
only in this age but also in the one to come.
And He put all things in subjection under His
feet, and gave Him as head over all things to the
church,
which is His body, the fullness of Him who
fills all in all. [Ephesians 1:18-23]

God's majesty is shocking in its superiority. It invades our hearts and minds and will not let us go until we bow the knee. If we do not surrender to sovereignty, we can have no authority. Our lives internally have to submit to Lordship. A warrior knows though, that it means more than that. It means every fight is eminently winnable because God's nature as an overcomer declares that probability constantly.

Majesty means we enter problem situations knowing that victory is inevitable. There are times when the Spirit of God is so powerfully present, all we have to do to win is avoid even the possibility of defeat. Sometimes we don't even need to fight, standing is all that is required [2 Chronicles 20:17; Ephesians 6:13].

There is a glorious inevitability about the Lord Jesus and the victory He won on Calvary [2 Corinthians 2:14; 1 Corinthians 15:57]. We will not fulfill our destiny outside of displays of God's sovereignty. Are we in danger of becoming triumphalistic? Let us hope so. Better to be in danger from a mind set on the Spirit, than on one which allows the possibility of defeat.

Triumphalism or fatalism — take your choice. A warrior knows that it is better to die thinking we can win, than to live knowing we cannot.

Majesty reveals glory. When glory comes, extreme joy follows with it. Warriors want to know the feel of a spirit of glory and of God resting upon them. Majesty provides the turning point in a potential disaster. If our mind is set on God's splendor, then we will overcome. Warriors want to take territory. Surpassing greatness is what they long to experience.

The dilemma of what we are going to choose to believe is actually of far greater concern than the matter itself. James knew that crisis would produce endurance and patience [James 1:34]. We will learn more about God's goodness and sovereignty through battle than through peace.

A warrior knows how to access the secret place of God's Presence.

> *For in the day of trouble He will conceal me in His tabernacle; In the secret place of His tent He will hide me; He will lift me up on a rock. And now my head will be lifted up above my enemies around me, And I will offer in His tent sacrifices with shouts of joy; I will sing, yes, I will sing praises to the LORD.*
> *[Psalm 27:5-6]*

It is vital to know God's heart for us personally in a time of trouble. We cannot fall from such grace. We practice being with God in our devotions. We learn to access the secret place through intimacy. Our inner certainties reveal our confidence in God or our unbelief. Rejoicing is the key to favor. Thanksgiving is a prelude to faith. Shouts of joy at God's supremacy are mandatory.

Spiritual warriors have a persistence in the Spirit. We can tell the quality of someone's inner life by the amount of opposition it takes to discourage them. This was one way that I determined the current readiness to fight of people that I mentored. The enemy needs to work harder against us this year than he did the last; otherwise we are not growing. Majesty, by definition, always increases. From glory to glory. God is irrepressible and indomitable. He cannot be overcome.

Spiritual warriors have a steadfast, unyielding quality that the world would call stubbornness and ruthless behavior. This can be mistaken for arrogance or not caring, by people of lesser spiritual caliber who vacillate between truth and compromise on their purpose.

Warriors get rid of every weight and anything that slows them down. This may make them unpopular people to be around at times. A guy in a previous church wanted to come on a missions trip I was organizing. Our purpose was to bring breakthrough to a particular church in eastern Europe. It was not a trip for the fainthearted, and I knew that he had not passed his own personal tests. I would not let him come. We would be babysitting him while trying to get a breakthrough. He would be a handicap we did not need.

Ruthless? — possibly. Arrogant? — not at all. It would have been arrogant to have taken him. Rookies are chosen by God not men. David, as a very young man, could be chosen as Goliath's opponent because God's hand was upon him. However, he also had to have some mileage in warfare in the shape of a lion and a bear. A warrior has his heart centered on majesty and fixed to the internal compass of persistent alignment with the Lord.

Warriors know that sovereignty can turn everything around and work things in our favor.

> *And we know that God causes all things to work together for good to those who love God, to those who are called according to His purpose.*
> *For those whom He foreknew, He also predestined to become conformed to the image of His Son, so that He would be the firstborn among many brethren;*
> *and these whom He predestined, He also called; and these whom He called, He also justified; and these whom He justified, He also glorified.*
> *What then shall we say to these things? If God is for us, who is against us?*
> *[Romans 8:28-31]*

The Father uses everything for our good. Our part is firstly to love God in our circumstances. In this way we are not distracted by events, but fully focused on Who the Lord is for us. Secondly, we need to remain in line with our calling and purpose, as our situation unfolds. In this way, we may determine the particular significance of our circumstances in relation to our training or the warfare in which we are engaged.

Everything has a purpose, and the intention of God is that we are always in a position to understand His glory. The Father's intention is to bring many sons into glory [Hebrews 2:10]. Glory is about majesty, understanding and reveling in the supremacy of the Lord. Glory too, is always connected with majestic inevitability. All things work together for good as we cooperate with God's purposes. This is not Christian fatalism. We are yoked in partnership with Jesus. We are choosing to abide in Jesus no matter the circumstances or the provocation from the enemy. If we allow the enemy to reduce us to carnality in our life issues on a regular basis then we remain untrained and untried for the highest level.

If we remain untested by life, we will be unfit for battle. An athlete who trains poorly, races badly. James understood this, as did all the apostles.

> *Consider it all joy, my brethren, when you encounter various trials,*
> *knowing that the testing of your faith produces endurance.*

And let endurance have its perfect result, so that you may be perfect and complete, lacking in nothing.
But if any of you lacks wisdom, let him ask of God, who gives to all generously and without reproach, and it will be given to him.
But he must ask in faith without any doubting, for the one who doubts is like the surf of the sea, driven and tossed by the wind.
For that man ought not to expect that he will receive anything from the Lord,
being a double-minded man, unstable in all his ways. [James 1:2-8]

There is a difference between warfare and adversity. Warfare is full-on demonic attack perpetrated by evil spirits or human agents of demonic powers. Adversity involves the trials and tests of everyday life and circumstances.

For us to become Christlike, we need events and situations that are a test for our spirituality. Trials enable us to put away our carnality and receive Jesus into areas of our life where He can change our character and personality. The fruit of the spirit both support and challenge our spirituality.

But the fruit of the Spirit is love, joy, peace, patience, kindness, goodness, faithfulness, gentleness, self-control; against such things there is no law.

Now those who belong to Christ Jesus have crucified the flesh with its passions and desires.

If we live by the Spirit, let us also walk by the Spirit. [Galatians 5:22-25]

If we are to grow in patience then we will need some trying people and circumstances. Our joy is tested almost every day. We have to work at our peace (labor to enter into rest) [Hebrews 4:11], and we must practice love constantly. Self-control is a necessity if we are to overthrow the enemy.

Most trials and tests are teaching us more than one thing. Every circumstance provides an opportunity for Christlike behavior to emerge. The warriors who understand and practice this become good at passing tests and are able to grow quickly and properly.

Warriors do not look for sympathy; they look for majesty. If you require pity from other people, you are living in the wrong place. God will give you compassion if you need it. He is your Comforter — otherwise, stop whining and get on with your training. Pick yourself up and get back in the fight.

The Father's intention in developing you is to produce endurance, increase your faith, make you mature so that you lack nothing, and pass you fit for battle. The question for a warrior is therefore: "What am I doing, and is it compatible with God's purpose?" Adversity is training for reigning. It is designed to equip us for a fight and provide, under pressure, what we need in order to prosper in a conflict.

The Father has designed our path in advance [Romans 8:29-30]. We are learning to live an intentional life within that plan. When we know our identity, destiny, and calling; then we discover the faith, character, and lifestyle we must pursue as citizens of heaven on earth. All trials and tests are designed to produce that person. Our response then to trials? "If God is for us, who can be against us?" The enemy does not want to go up against God; he wants to go up against us! The enemy is defeated by Christ in us. Jesus needs to be present in our lives in a way that produces consternation and fear in the enemy.

Warriors seek to wear the enemy down, to debilitate him. We do that by staying fresh. The Lord's ability to strengthen and inspire us with His lovingkindness never ceases. His capacity to comfort us never fails on any occasion. Ask for it; ask for it! With God everyday we start afresh. His purpose and provision is new every morning [Lamentations 3:21-25]. The faithfulness of God is astounding and it is the very foundation of our confidence and expectation. Always trust God to be majestic.

Though our outer man is having a tough day, our inner man is being renewed each day in the majesty of God [2 Corinthians 4:16]. Our inner man adapts to the Presence of God; our outer man is diverted by circumstances. Change a crisis into a turning point.

Warriors recognize the hand of God behind the work of the enemy. No matter what the enemy is doing, the Father is working to freely give us all things and to add to our Christlikeness. All things that the enemy will use against us, God will use for us — if not initially, always eventually. Some battles are won quickly; major battles are won over time. Stay fresh — the enemy hates it.

Stalemates occur when further progress is impossible. The enemy does not have to defeat us to win. He just has to stop us. We get bogged down when we allow ourselves to become stale. When we stay fresh we are more focused. Our rejoicing is sharp and crisp. Our faith is bright. We force the enemy to work, and all the time we are becoming more like Jesus. When the enemy starts to lose ground on several fronts, he will quit. If we are stale, it is our lack of majesty that makes us so. In majesty, we are expecting to overcome. There is no way we can lose. Our rejoicing maintains our freshness. We are learning progressively to stay fresher, longer.

Warriors are responsive towards God, not reactive to their circumstances. We accept everything as being from the hand of God and therefore for our benefit, regardless of the initial source. We know that Jesus reigns. We know that God allows in His wisdom what He can easily prevent by His power. We cannot be intimated by the enemy because we are too busy being fascinated by Jesus.

Warriors see everything as an opportunity to grow, to learn, and to increase faith. We are not avoiding tough situations because we are learning to extract from them everything we can in order to advance. We are not looking for rescue; we are more interested in God being glorified. Warriors fight from victory, not towards it. That means that every situation is not ours to win; it's ours to lose.

If we remain in Christ — alert, ready, and focused — we cannot lose. Everything leads to majesty. If the enemy succeeds in separating us from the reality of Christ within, he wins. There is a place in the Spirit set aside for us where we make the enemy confused. We weary him by our rest. We discourage him by our faith. We demoralize him by our joy. We depress him by our endurance. He is dispirited by our favor, defeated by our grace.

True warriors feed on the faithfulness of God. Full salvation produces total victory. Warriors never make allowances for losing; they make plans to win.

Assignment

❈ How are you embracing crisis … what is the purpose behind the difficulties you are facing currently?

❈ What is your response to warfare and adversity? For what conflict is God training you?

❀ Where in your life do you need to be refilled with the Holy Spirit and develop some freshness in Christ?

Commission

❀ What is your present experience of majesty? What attitude must you cultivate in order to increase your anointing to overcome?

❀ Work through your current circumstances with the Holy Spirit, asking Him for wisdom to align them with the purposes and benefits of God.

Personal Notes

Conclusion

God wants the pleasure of our company; that's why He created us in the first place. He wants us to live in His presence, forever. Like Joshua, who Exodus 33:11 notes *"did not depart from the tabernacle"* where Moses and God talked face-to-face, spiritual warriors are called to remain in the presence of God. Joshua's confidence in God's nature helped him time and again on the battlefield as the Israelites took the Promised Land.

We need to understand that every situation has been designed for us to discover more of God's presence and find access to even deeper levels. Confidence is the gateway to that presence. Our belonging there is part of our inheritance in Christ.

The word "warrior" conjures up images of violence and conflict, but a spiritual warrior is essentially peaceful, untroubled, and restful. Remaining calm is vital to the internal power and anointing that helps those around us overcome the enemy in their own lives. Warriors are dedicated, focused, committed, disciplined, and operate with a clear vision in mind. They have an internal compass that keeps them pointed toward the will of God. They keep moving in the same direction that God has challenged them to go—no matter what. Every champion in Scripture moved from crisis to crisis, but did so with the confidence that God was with him. Spiritual warriors, in every generation since Adam and Eve were created, live out the call of 2 Corinthians 6:4-10—

> *But in all things we commend ourselves as ministers of God: in much patience, in tribulations, in needs, in distresses, in stripes, in imprisonments, in tumults, in labors, in sleeplessness, in fastings; by purity, by knowledge, by longsuffering, by kindness, by the Holy Spirit, by sincere love, by the word of truth, by the power of God, by the armor of righteousness on the right hand and on the left, by honor and dishonor, by evil report and good report; as deceivers, and yet true; as unknown, and yet well known; as dying, and behold we live; as chastened, and yet not killed; as sorrowful, yet always rejoicing; as poor, yet making many rich; as having nothing, and yet possessing all things.*

That is the mission of the spiritual warrior.

Other Books by Graham Cooke

- ❈ A Divine Confrontation... Birth Pangs of the New Church
- ❈ Developing Your Prophetic Gifting
- ❈ The Nature of God
- ❈ Hiddenness and Manifestation
- ❈ Crafted Prayer
- ❈ Beholding and Becoming
- ❈ Toward a Powerful Inner Life
- ❈ The Language of Promise
- ❈ God's Keeping Power
- ❈ Living in Dependency and Wonder
- ❈ The Prophetic Equipping Series, Volume 1— Approaching the Heart of Prophecy
- ❈ The Prophetic Equipping Series, Volume 2— Prophecy and Responsibility
- ❈ Way of The Warrior Series, Volume 1— Qualities of a Spiritual Warrior
- ❈ Way of The Warrior Series, Volume 2— Manifesting Your Spirit
- ❈ Way of The Warrior Series, Volume 3—Coming into Alignment

Co-Authored

- ❈ Permission Granted
- ❈ When Heaven Opens

About the Author

Graham Cooke is part of The Mission core leadership team, working with senior team leader, David Crone, in Vacaville, California. Graham's role includes training, consulting, mentoring, and being part of a think tank to examine the journey from present to future.

He is married to Theresa who has a passion for worship and dance. She loves to be involved in intercession, warfare, and setting people free. She cares about injustice, abuse, and has compassion on people who are sick, suffering, and disenfranchised.

They have six children and one grandchild. Ben and Seth [32 and 30] both reside and work in the UK. Ben is developing as a writer, is very funny, and probably knows every movie ever made. Seth is a musician, a deep thinker with a caring outlook and amazing capacity for mischief.

Sophie-Marie, and son-in-law Mark, both oversee the daily operation of Brilliant Book House. They are a warm-hearted, friendly, deeply humorous couple with lots of friends. They have played a significant part in Graham's ministry by developing the resources, running the store, and developing new products. Their daughter, Evelyn-Rose (August 2006) is a delight — a happy little soul who likes music, loves to dance, and enjoys books.

Daughters Alexis and Alyssa live in Sacramento. Alexis is loving, kind, and gentle. She is very intuitive and steadfast toward her friends. Alyssa is a very focused and determined young woman who is fun-loving with a witty sense of humor.

Also, Graham and Theresa have two beautiful young women, Julianne and Megan, both in Australia, who are a part of their extended family.

Graham is a popular conference speaker and is well-known for his training programs on the prophetic, spiritual warfare, intimacy and devotional life, leadership, spirituality, and the church in transition. He functions as a consultant and free thinker to businesses, churches, and organizations, enabling them to develop strategically. He has a passion to establish the Kingdom and build prototype churches that can fully reach a post-modern society.

A strong part of Graham's ministry is in producing finances and resources to the poor and disenfranchised in developing countries. He supports many projects specifically for widows, orphans, and people in the penal system. He hates abuse of women and works actively against human trafficking and the sex slave trade, including women caught up in prostitution and pornography.

If you would like to invite Graham to minister at an event, please complete our online Ministry Invitation Form at www.grahamcooke.com.

If you wish to become a financial partner for the sake of missions and compassionate acts across the nations, please contact his office at office@grahamcooke.com where his personal assistant, Jeanne Thompson, will be happy to assist you.

Graham has many prayer partners who play a significant part in supporting his ministry through intercession and sponsorship. Prayer partners have the honor to be Graham's shield. They are his defensive covering that allows him to advance the Kingdom all over the world. The partners are a vital part of Graham's interdependent team. If you are interested in becoming a prayer partner, please contact his international coordinator, Pam Jarvis, at prayer@grahamcooke.com.

You may contact Graham by writing to:

Graham Cooke
6391 Leisure Town Road
Vacaville, California
USA 95687
www.grahamcooke.com

Brilliant Book House

Brilliant Book House is a California-based publishing company founded and directed by Graham Cooke and is dedicated to producing high-quality Christian resources and teaching materials. Brilliant Book House seeks to equip all of our readers to lead brilliant lives, confidently led by the Holy Spirit into the destiny God has for you.

We believe you have a unique call on your life that can only be found in God. He has something for you that is far beyond your wildest dreams. As you step out into that purpose, we want to stand with you, offering you encouragement, training, and hope for your journey. We want to equip you for what God wants to do in you, and through you. That is our promise to you.

Brilliant is the culmination of a longtime dream of our founder, Graham Cooke. A thinker and a strategist, Graham is also a builder with a particular desire to establish resource churches that are prophetic, progressive and supernatural. Brilliant Book House is a key part of that call—producing books, journals, MP3s, e-books, DVDs, CDs, and other teaching materials. For more on Graham, visit www.grahamcooke.com.